D0363844

I Am, Therefore I Think

I Am, Therefore I Think

*Philosophers Answer Your Questions
About Love, Nothingness,
and Everything Else . . .*

Edited by Alexander George

SCEPTRE

Copyright © 2007 by Alexander George

First published in Great Britain in 2007 by Hodder & Stoughton
A division of Hodder Headline

The right of Alexander George to be identified as the Author of
the Work has been asserted by him in accordance with
the Copyright, Designs and Patents Act 1988.

A Sceptre Book

3

A CIP catalogue record for this title is available from the British Library

Hardback ISBN 9780340937891

Typeset in Rotis Serif by Hewer Text UK Ltd, Edinburgh
Printed and bound by Clays Ltd, St Ives plc

Hodder Headline's policy is to use papers that are natural, renewable
and recyclable products and made from wood grown in sustainable
forests. The logging and manufacturing processes are expected to
conform to the environmental regulations of the country of origin.

Hodder & Stoughton Ltd
A division of Hodder Headline
338 Euston Road
London NW1 3BH

Contents

Introduction

'Don't let yourself get overwhelmed with questions; just take it easy.'

– Ludwig Wittgenstein, *Notebooks 1914–1916*

Homo Philosophicus

There is a paradox about philosophy: it is both everywhere and nowhere.

Philosophy is everywhere because each of us, throughout life, confronts philosophical issues. Whether these be of the urgent variety ('Would it be wrong to steal a kiss?') or, instead, of the kind that quietly ties your mind in knots while you lie in bed ('If God knows everything, then am I free to decide when to get up?'), philosophical questions are our constant companions. From nursery to nursing home, we never cease to think and talk about philosophical issues. It may be doubtful how sapient humans actually are, but it is not debatable how unstoppably philosophical we are: our species would have been better named *Homo philosophicus*.

That philosophy's omnipresence is not common knowledge is itself a manifestation of our central paradox. Most people do not realise that many of the questions they have been mulling over on their own or in the company of friends are at the very root of philosophy. When I was small, my father asked me what happens when an unstoppable force meets an unmovable object. I felt there had to be an answer and mentally squirmed every which way to find it. (My father, in response to my pestering, eventually said something about limbo, and I remember asking myself when I would be old enough to understand that key concept.) When pursued doggedly and creatively enough, such common questions grow into the grandest of philosophical systems. But few people realise this, because philosophy is rarely taught in schools and, though it is usually available at the university level, many people have no access to such higher education. Those who do are hesitant to take a philosophy course – often precisely because philosophical writing was something they had not been introduced to when young. In this sense, philosophy is nowhere.

The net effect of philosophy's simultaneous ubiquity and absence is that, while people might often stand to profit from access to the philosophical tradition, they are largely denied it.

This situation is all the more lamentable given philosophy's inherently open nature. Anyone can play. Tradition and pedigree count for little: a position's interest and justification are what matter. And unlike many other areas of great human endeavour, philosophy does not require equipment, instruments, laboratories or field work in order to gain entry or to contribute. Philosophy's start-up costs are as low as they come.

The website AskPhilosophers.org was created to relieve this paradox. Scores of philosophers have volunteered to place their talents as teachers and scholars at the public service. The response has been overwhelming, with thousands of questions flooding in from all corners of the planet. From young children to the elderly, from doctors and lawyers to those untouched by education, from the hyper-articulate to those piecing together what little English they know to formulate their questions. What you have before you is a selected compilation of a fraction of the stimulating questions and answers that have appeared on the website. They have been roughly organised by topic. These topics have themselves been loosely grouped together under the four resonant questions that the great German philosopher Immanuel Kant thought were central to philosophy. Of course, for all their variety, ingenuity and humour, these exchanges in no way exhaust the sorts of questions and answers these topics have given rise to; they do not pretend to be more than a sampling of the kinds of reflections that are at home in philosophy. We inhabit a strange world, we are ourselves peculiar creatures, and our relationships to that world and to one another are themselves often bafflingly mysterious. Fodder for philosophy is everywhere.

Any relief from our paradox is necessarily moderate, however. Despite technological wizardry there has been no advance, as far as philosophy is concerned, on Socrates' practice of face-to-face conversation with another person. Still, I hope some relief will be judged better than none. If these questions and answers can provide some insight and direction to our thinking, if they can help bring a few questioning minds into stimulating contact with the wonders of a grand tradition of human reflection, if they can convince some curious but hesitant souls that philosophy is not for the brilliant or the other-worldly but rather simply for the thinking person, which is to say for everyone, then something valuable will have been accomplished after all.

Alexander George
Amherst, Massachusetts

Part I

What Can I Know?

'We imbibe an archaic natural philosophy with our mother's milk. In the fullness of time, what with catching up on current literature and making some supplementary observations of our own, we become clearer on things. But the process is one of growth and gradual change: we do not break with the past, nor do we attain to standards of evidence and reality different in kind from the vague standards of children and laymen. Science is not a substitute for common sense, but an extension of it. The quest for knowledge is properly an effort simply to broaden and deepen the knowledge which the man in the street already enjoys, in moderation, in relation to the commonplace things around him. To disavow the very core of common sense, to require evidence for that which both the physicist and the man in the street accept as platitudinous, is no laudable perfectionism; it is a pompous confusion, a failure to observe the nice distinction between the baby and the bath water.'

– W. V. Quine, 'The Scope and Language of Science'

Q

❝ *Is there such a thing as Nothing? We can say that socks are in the drawer or that nothing is. But if nothing can be in the drawer, then Nothing must exist in some way. But if so, does it occupy the same space at the same time as those things that aren't Nothing?* **❞**

A

Alexander George: How many hands do you have? Two? Or do you have three? Your left hand, your right hand, and the non-existent third hand that's attached to your head?

Obviously, that last 'hand' shouldn't count. To say that you don't have a third hand isn't to say that you have a hand that possesses the property of non-existence. We get ourselves into a real muddle if we take claims of non-existence to mean that there is some object that has the property of non-existence, for then that object must both exist (to have any properties whatsoever) and not exist, and that can't be. So when we say that no one came to the party, we mean to deny that someone came to the party – not to affirm that at least one person did (namely 'no one', the 'non-person', the person with the rather anti-social property of non-existence).

This confusion becomes unavoidable if one assumes that every noun in a language must refer to something. For if you do, when you come upon a sentence like 'Nothing beats a royal flush' you'll be forced to conclude that something does after all beat a royal flush, namely Nothing. But not all nouns contribute to the meaning of sentences in the same way. In particular, some (like 'nothing') don't refer to anything, while others (like 'Manhattan') do.

Therefore, it's a confusion to think of Nothing as something that's jockeying with something for the same space. In any given space, either there's something or there isn't. And if there isn't anything there, if there's nothing there, that doesn't mean that there's actually something there, namely some thing called 'Nothing'.

Q

66 *Doesn't the existence of something in one's imagination at the very least give that thing a semblance of actuality?* **99**

A

Alexander George: OK, so I'm now imagining the winning lottery ticket in my wallet. Let me check. [Pause.] Damn. Not even close to being a winner. In fact, there's not even a lottery ticket.

We might speak of a bucket of diamonds existing 'in one's imagination'. But this doesn't mean that the bucket of diamonds actually resides in some wispy way in one's mind. If anything does exist in one's mind, it's the thought of the bucket of diamonds, or perhaps an image of it. But not the bucket itself.

But we are very close to a Grand Philosophical Headache: understanding what makes that thought or that image *about* the thing it's about. This is especially puzzling when the thing it's about doesn't actually exist at all.

A

Peter Lipton: I can imagine a mountain made of pure gold without that mountain's existing, even a little bit. But it may well be that my act of imagination entails that something else must exist, namely the cause of that act.

Descartes used this line of thought for one of his arguments for the existence of God. He had an idea of God, and he thought that the idea must have a cause, and that the only possible cause in this case is God Himself. Why? Because a cause must have at least as much 'reality' as its effect, and only God has as much reality as the idea of God. Not, it must be said, a very convincing argument to modern eyes: why can't big ideas have small causes?

Q

66 *Our eight-year-old son said yesterday that all things have opposites. He was discussing the matter with our daughter, who is ten, and she argued that this cannot be so. The examples our son provided were of the kind: light versus dark, day versus night, cold versus hot.*

Our daughter then raised the question: what is the opposite of a banana?

What should I have answered? Is there really a duality in all things and, if so, how does it apply to the banana case? **99**

A

Jyl Gentzler: When my daughter was very young, she had a book called *My First Look at Opposites* (Dorling Kindersley, 1990). It taught her words such as 'big' and 'little', 'thick' and 'thin', 'long' and 'short', through colourful photographs of big and little dolls, thick and thin ropes, and long and short candles. Surprisingly, she picked up these concepts very quickly. I say 'surprisingly', because as a matter of fact, the phenomenon of opposites is very complex. We use opposite terms when we are comparing objects and noting their differences. Often we make this comparative function explicit by adding the suffixes '-er' and '-est'. But even when we don't use these suffixes, we are still implicitly making comparisons when we use these terms.

Let's take 'poor' and 'rich'. People whom we characterise as poor within a particular context are markedly different with respect to wealth from those whom we characterise as rich within the same context. I mention the importance of context, because in different contexts, and for the purposes of different comparisons, we may pick out the same person as rich and as poor. In his small village in the Andes, Juan is rich; in comparison to those who live on the Upper East Side, he is poor. Mary is richer than Juan, but Mary is the poorest resident of the Upper East Side. Is Mary rich or poor? Well, it depends on the wealth of the person to whom one is implicitly comparing Mary. In different contexts, there are different ranges represented on the spectrum of wealth, and when you locate Mary on this range, she may fall at different ends, either at the end that we designate (for comparative purposes) as poor or at the end that we designate as rich.

So when we characterise two objects by using opposite terms, we're saying that these objects are very different from one another, in at least a certain respect, in at least a particular context. When we characterise a single object by using one of these terms, we are nonetheless making an implicit comparison: we are saying that within a particular context that we have in mind, this object would fall at one end on a range of a particular way of being.

What about 'banana' then? Does this term also have an opposite in the sense in which 'rich' has an opposite in 'poor'? 'Banana' isn't obviously a comparative term: something isn't more or less of a banana; and, unlike the poor and the rich, bananas are correctly designated as bananas regardless of the context in which one is designating them as such. But perhaps matters are a bit more complex than this disanalogy might suggest. Surely we can compare bananas to other objects, and surely, some objects are much more similar to bananas than to other objects. Could there be a type of object that is an opposite to banana in the sense of being most different from a banana?

I'm inclined to say that, no, a banana does not have an opposite in this sense. Notice that when we compare objects like lions and bananas, we don't compare every aspect of them at the same time. I can compare a lion and a banana with respect to size ('big' and 'little'), or with respect to a propensity to make noise ('noisy' and 'quiet'), or with respect to their opacity (both are opaque), and they count as similar in some respects and different in others. Whether I regard them as very similar or very different in these respects would depend on the context in which I was comparing them. Yes, a lion is big in comparison to a banana, but it is small in comparison to the Earth. If I were comparing the size of a lion to the size of a banana, the Earth, and the Solar System, I would count both the lion and banana as small; if I were to compare only them, then in the context that I am implicitly assuming, I would say that a lion is big and a banana is small. There is no object that counts as an opposite to a banana in the sense that it stands on the opposite end of the spectrum for *any* property that a banana has, in *whichever* context that one might be making the comparison.

Perhaps, though, 'banana' has an opposite in the same way that 'day' has the opposite 'night'. 'Night' and 'day' do indeed designate things that are commonly regarded as opposites, and these terms, like 'banana', do not have any common comparative forms: it's never more or less day or night, even though the boundary between day and night is itself indefinite. Does anything serve as an opposite to 'banana', as 'night' serves as an opposite to 'day'? I think so. 'Night' and 'day' are exhaustive as well as exclusive – if it's not day, then it's night. Now, the only thing that is opposite to 'banana' in this sense is 'not-banana'! Admittedly, 'not-banana' is a word that we rarely have occasion to use, but that can't stop us from correctly claiming that you and I (and the Eiffel Tower) have something in common, namely we're all not-bananas.

Q

66 *I believe that I am the only thing that really exists. How can anyone prove to me that he or she really exists?* 99

A

Peter Lipton: Your question reminds me of the story Bertrand Russell once told about the philosopher who claimed that solipsism – the view that only you exist, or anyway that there is no reason to believe anyone else exists – was obviously correct and she couldn't understand why everyone else didn't agree with her!

But there does seem to be a sense in which you cannot prove that anyone other than you exists. In that sense, it also seems that you can't prove that you existed in the past or will exist in the future. So if you have standards this high, then the most you know is the content of your current experience (e.g., that you're now perceiving something red), though even this may be saying too much.

Q

« Do ideas exist independently of us, out there in the ether, waiting to be discovered?

For instance, did the idea of the motor car exist, say, 1,000 years ago, before any human ever thought of it? »

A

Joseph G. Moore: Discovered things exist independently of their discovery (think of uninhabited islands and rare species), while invented things come into existence in the very process of their invention (think of the first light bulb). But even if the first light bulb came into existence when Edison invented it, what about the *idea* of the light bulb? Did Edison invent this at the same time, or was it, as you suggest, hanging around for eons just waiting for Edison or some other genius to stumble upon it?

It's a great question, and connected at root to venerable metaphysical puzzles which, in my view, are still unresolved. In fact, it's really the question that troubled Plato 2,400 years ago. The issue isn't so much how we use the concepts of invention and discovery (though this is interesting), but rather the unsettled status of the 'ideas' that we discover/invent.

We often talk as if ideas transcend the particular, spatially and temporally located episodes of thinking in which they figure. We say: Newton and Leibniz came up with the idea of the calculus independently of one another. And in saying this we seem to hold that one and the same idea (or set of ideas) existed and was at work both when Newton entertained it *and* at the different time and place that Leibniz did. We further detach ideas from particular mental events when we say: 'Democracy is a great idea that's difficult to implement,' or perhaps even 'The idea of anonymous sex is more appealing than the reality.' Or better yet: 'No one has come up with an idea that will solve global suffering, but one must exist.'

If we take our idea-talk seriously and straightforwardly, we seem committed to ideas as things that exist independently of the particular episodes of thinking that involve them. But where and when do these ideas exist? Always and everywhere? Outside of space and time? In some Platonic heaven, or mysterious ether? No answer seems palatable, but without one we can't hope to understand how ideas come to figure in our thought and talk about them.

A similar puzzle plagues numbers: we talk as if numbers are distinct from the symbols such as '2', and 'π' that we use to pick them out. For instance, when we erase the equation '2+5 = 7' on the blackboard, we don't destroy the number 2! And likewise, numbers are distinct from any mental ideas I might have about them: when I die, the numbers won't die with me! But then where, when and how do numbers exist? And how do we interact with them? Our puzzle also connects to the ancient problem of universals: we seem to talk as if there are properties, such as redness, that exist independently of particular red things, such as my son's tricycle and the rose I just gave my wife (honestly). But then where, when and how does the universal property of redness exist? And how do the tricycle and rose partake of it?

But now I've gotten long on rhetoric and short on argument. Suffice it to say that, in my view, your question is still unsettled and unsettling. Anyone who truly loves metaphysics will agree, as will anyone who truly loathes it.

Q

❝ *The movie* The Matrix *depicts a world in which we are all connected to a giant computer. This computer sends sensory signals directly to our brains, making us believe that we live in a fairly normal world. We seem to have sensations of office buildings, night clubs, and the other everyday aspects of life in the big city. As Neo soon discovers, though, the real world is nothing like the mundane experiences we have when we're connected to the Matrix.*

Is this scenario – or one along these lines – possible? Couldn't the sensory signals we interpret as being from the world really be from, say, a machine? Can this possibility be proven wrong? **❞**

A

Matthew Silverstein: Most philosophers agree that the scenario depicted in *The Matrix* is at least *possible*. But as long as we're talking about possibility, the situation might be even more alarming than the one depicted in the movie. At least in the film we're all sharing the same, collective hallucination. It might be the case, however, that you're *the only one* plugged into the Matrix! Perhaps you don't even have a full body; you could be just a brain floating in a vat of nutrients and connected to a computer that is feeding you electrochemical signals.

In his *Meditations*, Descartes famously considers an even more radical possibility: the entire material world could be an illusion. You could be a disembodied ghost dreaming that you have a body or a disembodied mind being deceived by a malicious and powerful demon into believing that material objects exist.

Philosophers usually discuss outlandish thought experiments such as these in order to raise questions about the possibility of knowledge. If knowledge requires absolute certainty, and if you can't rule out the possibility (however minute) that you're a brain in a vat, then you can't know something even as elementary as whether you have a body. If knowledge does *not* require certainty, scenarios like the one in *The Matrix* still pose all sorts of troubling problems. After all, it's not clear what would even count as a good reason for you to believe that you're not a brain in a vat!

Q

66 Can machines have knowledge? 99

A

Louise Antony: Clearly, machines can process information. For the machine to have knowledge, however, this information has to be information 'for' the machine – i.e., the machine must *understand* the information it processes. What would that involve?

In the first place, the states or events in the machine that store or process the information (including, for example, databases and programs) would have to be richly integrated with all the other states of the machine, in particular with the machine's input and output states, analogously to the way in which our thoughts and memories are integrated with our perceptions and motor commands. This requirement for machine understanding is a matter of how the machine is *organised functionally* – how its parts are put together relative to other parts, and to its inputs and outputs.

The second requirement is that the input states that supply the information be properly related to the states of affairs in the world the information is about. This is a *content requirement* – a requirement that says what's necessary for the machine's states to be genuinely meaningful. For human beings, the input states are perceptions, and what a visual perception 'means' – what it is about – is determined by lawful relations between the physical structure of the object under view, and the patterns of firing in the retinal cells receiving the signal. By contrast, in currently existing computers, the inputs, which are strings in an arbitrary symbol system, only have meaning in the sense that, and to the extent that, we, the users, assign meaning to them.

You may have heard of the Turing Test for machine intelligence. This is a criterion proposed by Alan Turing, the brilliant logician who laid the mathematical foundations for digital computers. Turing's idea was essentially this: have a person type questions to each of two 'respondents' at remote locations, one a computer, the other another human being. If, after some sufficiently long period of time, the interrogator cannot tell the difference between the machine and the human being, then the machine should count as intelligent.

The Turing Test clearly does not test for the relevant conditions. The test yields both false positives and false negatives: false positives because it could be passed by a radio-operated animatronic doll, and false negatives, because it would be failed by any minded creature who happened to be paralysed and unable to make any behavioural response. The right way to consider the question is to look beyond the behaviour of the machine to see if the best explanation of that behaviour is that its inner workings conform to the conditions given above.

Q

66 *What is truth? How can we ever know that we have attained it?* **99**

A

Richard Heck: Many of the most profound questions in philosophy are naturally expressed as questions about truth. And the question of what truth is, to be sure, is among the most profound questions in philosophy. There are several sorts of answers: A proposition is true if it corresponds to a 'fact' in the world; or if it coheres with the rest of what we believe; or if it serves our practical purposes; or if it can be verified on the basis of our most immediate experiences. But none of these views has yet won the day, and so some philosophers have been led to deny that truth is actually a very interesting property at all. We'll meet them shortly.

People can be led to ask the question what truth is for many different reasons. In this case, I take the worry to be: if truth is something really *ultimate*, then we can never really know if we've attained the truth. (I think that's not far from Pontius Pilate's reason for asking the question (John xviii, 38).) But while there certainly is a worry here, it's not really one that has anything to do with truth.

Truth is a property that some propositions have and some do not. It can be hard to tell in which camp a given proposition falls. But this much we can say. The proposition that Wittgenstein was Jewish is true if Wittgenstein was Jewish, and it is false if Wittgenstein was not Jewish. The proposition that Frege was Catholic is true if Frege was Catholic, and it is false if Frege was not Catholic. Some philosophers, called 'deflationists', think that's about all there is to be said about truth. They're the ones who think truth isn't a very interesting property. I'd disagree, but we can all agree that, even if what's just been said isn't *all* there is to be said about truth, it is *something* that there is to be said about truth.

In some sense, this observation – that, in general, the proposition that things are thus and so is true if, and only if, things are thus and so – already suggests that whether a proposition is true depends upon how things are in the world. For example, whether the proposition that Russell was German is true depends upon, well, whether Russell was German, and that's a question of how things are 'out there'.

So, that said, how can we know that we have ever attained the truth? The obvious way to interpret the question is: how can we know, say, whether it is true that Wittgenstein was Jewish? Given what has been said, however, the question whether it is true that Wittgenstein was Jewish is simply the question whether Wittgenstein was Jewish. Of course, there is a very large issue now in the vicinity: namely, the problem of skepticism, which raises the question whether we can know anything at all. But that's not really a question about truth. It's a question about knowledge.

Q

66 *Can you disprove the statement, 'Truth is relative'? Could it be absolute?* **99**

A

Richard Heck: There are lots of kinds of relativism, and some of them are relatively uncontroversial. Suppose I ask, 'Is Benny Hill funny?' It's not that people can't disagree or even argue about this, but we don't really think there's any reason people have to agree: it might just be that some people think he's funny and other people don't, and no one's ultimately right or ultimately wrong. It's just a matter of taste or, in this case, of one's sense of humour. So the truth of the statement 'Benny Hill is funny' is, in some way or other, relative to the person making the statement.

But there is a very extreme form of relativism according to which everything is relative: the truth of every statement is relative to the person making it. And it has always been objected to this extreme view that it is ultimately incoherent because, or so it would seem, the truth of the statement 'Truth is relative' cannot itself be relative to the person making it. Otherwise, extreme relativism might be true for you but not for me, in which case, well, it's not true for me. Let's spell that out a bit more.

Let us ask the question: to what exactly is truth supposed to be relative? The most familiar challenge to the most extreme form of relativism, the claim that all truth is relative, is straightforward and, to my mind, has never been adequately answered. It is that the truth of 'Truth is relative' had better not be relative. But we can spell the argument out a little more.

Question: relative to what? Answer the question as you wish. Whatever you tell me, I will introduce an explicit statement of the alleged condition. So if the answer is 'relative to cultural standards', I'll ask you to consider something like: Lying is impermissible, according to the predominant standards of culture X. I can't even make sense of the claim that *that* is true only relative to cultural standards. It's like trying to make sense of 'It's warm in Texas in Oklahoma'.

Note that no such argument could show that truth was not in some interesting sense relative *in some particular area*. The foregoing does not show, for example, that *moral* claims are not true only relative to cultural standards, since 'Lying is impermissible, according to the predominant standards of culture X' is (at least arguably) not a moral claim but one about the standards of a particular culture. What the argument purports to show is that there must be a level at which the truth is not relative to anything.

A

Peter Lipton: Philosophers disagree about this, but I do think there is such a thing as absolute truth.

We need to distinguish the question of truth from the question of knowledge. It may well be there is no such thing as 'absolutely certain knowledge', something we believe to be true and that we couldn't possibly be wrong about. But whether we can know an absolute truth for certain or not, there could be such a truth.

At the same time, we need to allow that there may be certain statements that are not absolutely true or absolutely false, because they do not have a crisp enough meaning. One way this might happen is if one of the words in the statement is vague. So, it may be that a statement like 'People with exactly 100 hairs on their head are bald' is neither absolutely true nor absolutely false. But it doesn't follow from this that there are no absolute truths, because it doesn't follow that every statement uses vague words.

There may be some areas where absolute truth is not to be had. Some people would say this about statements about ethics, others would say this about statements about beauty. But it doesn't follow that there are no areas where there is absolute truth.

So does this leave any plausible examples of an absolute truth? Here is one: 'There are trees in Oregon.' Not the most exciting statement, but it's true, and not just for me. It's just true, absolutely. I leave it to you to come up with more interesting examples.

Q

66 How do we know modern-day mathematics is correct? 99

A

Daniel J. Velleman: Mathematicians try to ensure correctness by never accepting a mathematical statement as true without a proof. Of course, it's always possible that a mathematician will make a mistake when writing or checking a proof, so even if a mathematician has proven a statement and the proof has been checked by other mathematicians, there is still a small chance that there is a subtle mistake somewhere in the proof. (It has occasionally happened that a flawed mathematical proof was accepted for years before the flaw was spotted. One famous example is Alfred Bray Kempe's 1879 proof of the Four Colour Theorem, which was accepted until Percy John Heawood pointed out an error in the proof in 1890.) So if you're looking for an absolute guarantee of correctness, I don't think you're going to find one.

But even if we ignore the problem of careless errors, there are other questions one could raise about whether or not a proof of a mathematical statement guarantees the truth of the statement. Usually a proof of one mathematical statement makes use of other mathematical statements, so one could ask how we know that *those* statements are true. Of course, they have proofs too, but those proofs depend on other statements, and so on. How does the whole process get started? Most mathematicians today consider the starting point to be the Zermelo-Frankel (ZF) axioms of set theory.

Can we be sure of the correctness of the ZF axioms? These axioms include, for example, an axiom saying that if two sets have the same elements then they are equal, and an axiom saying that the union of two sets is a set. Some people regard the axioms as so intuitively clear that it is reasonable to accept them as true without proof. Another approach would be to simply define 'correctness' in mathematics to mean 'provability from the ZF axioms'. But almost everyone would agree that if the axioms are found to be inconsistent, then they can't be correct, so one step toward ensuring the correctness of mathematics might be proving the consistency of the axioms. Early in the 20th century the German mathematician David Hilbert tried to find such a proof in an attempt to establish the correctness of mathematics. Unfortunately, the Austrian logician Kurt Gödel's famous Incompleteness Theorems, proven in 1931, show that Hilbert's project cannot be carried out.

Despite all these worries about the certainty of mathematics, I think it should be said that math does seem to have a higher degree of certainty than any other field of study. Physicists no longer consider Newton's laws of motion to be exactly correct, but Euclid's theorems are still considered correct after more than 2,000 years.

Q

66 *Is anything really impossible?* **99**

A

Alexander George: Philosophers often distinguish between different kinds of impossibilities. Some contemplated situations would conflict with the laws of logic: for instance, the state of affairs in which I am over thirty years old and not over thirty years old is one that conflicts with the law of logic that says that 'A and not-A' is false for every statement A. We might say that that state of affairs is *logically* impossible, or impossible *relative to the laws of logic.*

By contrast, some situations conflict only with the laws of physics: for instance, the state of affairs in which I am moving faster than the speed of light is not a possible one according to contemporary physics. It's one that is logically but not *physically* possible; it is impossible *relative to the laws of physics.*

Likewise, we might have situations that we would describe as impossible *relative to the laws of chemistry,* and so on. And perhaps, when someone suggests that your spouse is having an affair, you will find yourself exclaiming that it's impossible, meaning not that such perfidy is inconsistent with the laws of logic or physics, etc., but that it's incompatible with what you believe to be true about your spouse.

If this is the right way to think about impossibility, then nothing is impossible – *tout court*. A situation is possible or impossible only *relative to* certain assumptions. And relative to any given body of assumptions, many situations will be impossible.

Q

66 *Is there a logical reason why most people prefer their own opinions to someone else's?* **99**

A

Louise Antony: Here's a conceptual reason: if I 'preferred' your opinion to my own, in the sense of thinking it is more likely to be true than the one I currently hold, then I presumably would change my opinion to match yours, and your opinion would *become* mine.

A

Peter Lipton: On some subjects I do have a good reason to prefer my own opinions, say because I was there at the time and saw it with my own eyes. But consider philosophical opinions. Why do I bother to form my own opinions? Why don't I just agree with everything the famous American philosopher Hilary Putnam says, since he is so smart? That would save me a lot of time, and it might well increase the reliability of my opinions. Well, in the case of philosophy, I guess part of the answer is that we don't just care about maximising the chances of having the right answer: we also think there is a particular value to working things out for oneself.

Here is one more point that your question raises. Most of our opinions are not just our own opinions anyway, since almost everything we know we know because of what other people tell us. Philosophers argue over whether reason or experience is the primary source of knowledge; but at a certain level the answer is neither. Testimony or communication wins hands down. There is very little indeed that you know entirely on your own, without relying on what others tell you.

Q

66 *I was loading up to go on a trip the other day and asked my dad why he was taking a lot of extra stuff and he said: 'Just in case the unexpected happens.'*

So out of that comes my question: if you expect the unexpected, then doesn't that make the unexpected expected and the expected unexpected? 99

A

Peter Lipton: Even if you expect the unexpected, you may still be surprised. I took my Swiss Army knife along, because I expected the unexpected, but I was still surprised when I had to use it to free a hedgehog that got itself locked in the glove compartment of my car. People who believe that life is full of surprises are often right.

A

Alexander George: When someone says 'I expect the unexpected,' we might understand this remark as we do the claim 'I fathered someone fatherless.' That is, we might interpret him as meaning that he expects some event which he also does not expect. That does seem like a contradiction.

But isn't that to misunderstand what he's trying to say? What he expects is not some event (which he also doesn't expect); rather, what he expects is that he will not expect some event. His expectation applies not to an event but rather to his non-expectation of some event. What he expects is that there will be some event that he does not expect.

Such an expectation is a *second-order* expectation: it applies to his *first-order* non-expectation of some event. My expectation that a credit card bill will soon arrive is a first-order expectation because the object of the expectation is an event (that itself has nothing to do with expectations). My expectation that Melanie will expect me to pay for dinner is a second-order expectation because it's an expectation *about an expectation.*

That's why, as Peter Lipton says, 'Even if you expect the unexpected, you may still be surprised': what surprises you and what you expected are different things. You're surprised by the fact that there is a hedgehog in your glove compartment, but not surprised by the fact that something surprised you.

Q

I'm often impatient when people claim something to be 'obvious'. Is it wrong not to want to accept such claims? Isn't it logical to want justification for them?

A

Alexander George: There is an old story told about a great mathematician. He had just claimed in class that some result was obvious when a student raised her hand and expressed some uncertainty. The mathematician looked puzzled, then sat down and began to think. Minutes, then hours, went by while he was deep in thought. The class period was just about over when the mathematician raised his head and triumphantly proclaimed: 'Yes, I was right: it *is* obvious!'

The joke here is related to what makes your question a little odd. You seem to want a justification for some claim that is advanced as basic or obvious. But if the speaker takes the claim to be basic, then presumably she thinks it is less in need of defence than any considerations that she might offer for its justification. In other words, if she thinks she could provide a justification for a claim, then presumably she wouldn't take that claim to be basic or fundamental after all.

We can put this point another way, by reflecting on the nature of justification. Often, a justification consists of an argument, that is, a collection of premises (or starting assumptions) whose truth is believed to render some claim more probable. Now, an argument will fail to be persuasive if the hearer is not willing to accept its premises without further justification. So, in demanding a justification for something claimed to be obvious, you signal your willingness to accept something as obvious after all (namely, the premises of the justifying argument)! In calling for justification, one does not escape the need to take something to be obvious; one rather pushes the burden along to some claim that one is, for the moment at least, content to let stand.

Q

❝ *Is the phrase 'before the Big Bang' meaningless, since the Big Bang is the beginning of everything, including time?* **❞**

A

Marc Lange: I, too, have heard it said that the phrase 'before the Big Bang' is meaningless. One analogy I have heard drawn is between the phrase 'before the Big Bang' and the phrase 'more northerly than 90 degrees north latitude'. Just as the latter phrase refers to no real location on Earth, so the former phrase is supposed to refer to no real location in time. According to cosmology's current picture of the Big Bang (as I understand it), the analogy is apt. (Of course, that doesn't rule out the possibility of further scientific developments resulting in corrections to the theory of the Big Bang.)

It may seem unsatisfying to you that a scientific theory could just rule out as 'meaningless' a notion that appears to be perfectly sensible. Intuitively, it seems like the question 'What happened before the Big Bang?' ought to have an ordinary answer, rather than a cop-out answer like 'There is no such time.' However, the history of science is full of examples of questions that were once thought to have ordinary (although perhaps as yet undiscovered) answers but that later were discovered not to. These discoveries were not cop-outs.

Rather, they were consequences of well-confirmed scientific theories. For example, it was once believed that in order for a body to keep moving at a constant speed in a constant direction, something must continually be acting upon it; otherwise it would slow down and eventually stop. That seems like a sensible idea, based on our everyday experiences. However, Newton discovered that the question 'What keeps this body moving at a constant speed in a constant direction?' has no answer because it is based on a mistaken view. According to Newton's first law of motion, a body that is acted upon by no force at all will nevertheless keep moving uniformly; forces cause *accelerations* (changes in the speed and direction of motion), and motion at a constant speed in a constant direction involves no acceleration. Consequently, that motion could be maintained indefinitely, and would be maintained indefinitely in the absence of anything acting to change it. Perhaps science has discovered that the question 'What happened before the Big Bang?' is in this respect like the pre-Newtonian question 'What's keeping this body moving at a constant speed in a constant direction?'

Q

66 Just about every theory in the history of science has either been revised or wholly rejected. So isn't there ample evidence to think that all our present-day theories are false? How can we be so sure that science offers anything more than a set of beliefs, like religions or myths? 99

A

Peter Lipton: Later scientific theories often contradict the theories they replace. Does this mean that science is not in the truth business? There is a simple and much discussed argument for this conclusion. The argument is known as the 'pessimistic induction': all scientific theories more than say 200 years old are now known to be false, so it is likely that all present and future theories will eventually be found to be false as well. So much for getting the truth from science.

There are a number of responses those of us who do think science is in the truth business can give. We can quibble with the premise of the pessimistic induction: surely not *all* theories more than 200 years old are now known to be false. For example, we still believe the theory that the blood circulates around the body, and that theory is much more than 200 years old. But even if the premise is an exaggeration, lots of our best long-held theories are contradicted by what we now believe. For example, if Einstein is right about the nature of motion, then Newton was wrong. Sure, Newton makes pretty good predictions when the velocities of bodies are low, but even then the theory is, strictly speaking, incorrect. (And probably not just strictly speaking: the very concept of mass is different for Einstein than it is for Newton.)

Another reply to the pessimistic induction is to stress that saying science is in the truth business does not mean you have to say that current scientific theories are the truth, the whole truth, and nothing but the truth. It is enough if our theories are approximately true, and that the approximation is improving. So someone who thinks science is in the truth business can just admit that probably almost no theory was or will be completely true.

Here is one more possible response to the pessimistic induction. Does the fact that we have made mistakes in the past really make it more likely that we will make mistakes in the future? We have better instruments and more data now than we used to have. And anyway, we learn from our mistakes. So maybe the fact that we have constructed theories and then figured out where they go wrong actually makes it not less likely but *more* likely that future theories will be true!

Q

66 *Why are the laws of morality usually opposed to the ways of behaving encouraged by the laws of evolution? For example, most moral codes encourage monogamy while the theory of evolution says that natural selection will favour promiscuity.* **99**

A

Sharon Street: Happily for fans of fidelity, monogamy and morality have deeper evolutionary origins than you might think.

Imagine you're a primeval woman trying to decide between two primeval men. Suppose they're equal in strength, intelligence, resources, sense of humour, looks, and so on – with a single difference: one is a fickle, philandering Don Juan; the other is hankering to commit for life, with eyes for only you. Choose the philanderer, and you and your offspring will likely have to fend for yourselves. Choose Mr Fidelity, however, and you and your offspring will get all the care, attention and resources this man has to offer. You can see why natural selection is going to favour women who prefer Mr Fidelity, other things being equal: with his help, you'll have a better shot at leaving more descendants. The evolution of this preference among women, in turn, creates a corresponding selective pressure on men to *be* Mr Fidelity rather than Don Juan, as women increasingly spurn the attentions of the latter and go gaga over the former.

Now imagine you're a primeval man. You've got resources to invest (maybe a nice cave and great hunting skills) and you're choosing between two primeval women: Ms Promiscuous and Ms Fidelity. Choose the former, and you may end up unwittingly showering your valuable resources on other men's kids. Choose the latter, though, and there's no chance of that. You can see why natural selection is going to favour men who prefer to share their resources with Ms Fidelity and her offspring. The evolution of this preference among men, in turn, creates a corresponding selective pressure on women to *be* Ms Fidelity rather than Ms Promiscuous.

All this is greatly oversimplified, but you get the idea: natural selection can sometimes favour monogamy (as the mating strategies of beavers, pigeons and many other species illustrate). The same goes for morality more generally. You might think that in the struggle to survive and reproduce, nice guys and gals always finish last, but this is false. If altruistic individuals can find each other and work together, and if they can identify ruthlessly selfish individuals and punish and exclude them, then the altruists will be able to reap tremendous benefits of co-operation that are unavailable to the purely selfish. In this way, natural selection can strongly favour altruistic behaviour.

Life is never simple, however, for sometimes the most effective reproductive strategy is not to *be* the altruist or Mr or Ms Fidelity; it's rather to *seem to be* (perhaps even to yourself), while cheating a bit, or even a lot, on the side. So human nature is a very mixed bag. But the bottom line is that our moral nature has just as deep an evolutionary basis as our self-interested nature. And the philosopher David Hume's point must always be kept in mind: from observations about the kinds of creatures we *are*, nothing follows – at least not without a great deal more discussion – about the kinds of creatures we *ought* to be. What's 'best' from an evolutionary 'point of view' (not a real point of view at all) is by no means always what's best from *our* point of view. And it's *our* point of view that matters for ethics. So no cheating!

Q

66 *What would happen if natural selection were proved wrong? Wouldn't this show that our understanding of reality is relative? And if it is relative, how are we sure that the way we understand our surroundings is the correct one?*

I really need you to answer this question because I am afraid of devoting my life to something that later will prove completely wrong! **99**

A

Richard Heck: There have been many instances over the centuries in which well-confirmed scientific theories were later shown to be wrong. Usually, they weren't *simply* wrong. There was something they had right, but then it turned out that there were problems and a very different theory had to be introduced, often with a wholly different metaphysics. Natural selection, as well confirmed as it now seems, could turn out to be wrong.

So yes, our understanding of the world is no more guaranteed to be correct than was that of our forebears. That doesn't show that *how reality is* is 'relative', only that, as you rightly say, our *understanding* of reality is conditioned by the time and place in which we find ourselves.

There's a lot we don't know, and a lot we think we know but, in fact, don't.

But it doesn't follow that we don't have good reason to believe what we believe. We do. If we should come to have better reason to believe something else, then we will, if we are rational, believe that other thing. But until we do find better reason to believe something else, we should, well, believe what we have best reason to believe. That such-and-such a theory *might* one day be proven to be wrong isn't a reason not to believe it. If it were, then we'd have no reason to believe anything. And of course we do have such reason. Right now, for example, I have excellent reason to believe that I am typing a response to a question about philosophy, and we have excellent reason to believe that species evolve through natural selection.

Practically speaking, I'd advise you to stop worrying about turning out to have been wrong. Being right in the end isn't really what matters. Copernicus was wrong, and Newton was wrong, and Franklin was wrong. Nonetheless, they all made incredibly important contributions to our understanding of the world around us. We could hardly have the understanding we do today of cosmology, gravity, or electricity without their work.

Q

66 *Can there be an event that is entirely random?* **99**

A

Daniel J. Velleman: Consider flipping a fair coin. This seems random, in the sense that we don't seem to be able to predict the outcome. Half the time the coin comes up heads and half the time it's tails, and we don't know which it's going to be until it lands. But in another sense, it doesn't seem random at all: if you knew the speed at which the coin was spinning, its exact position above the table, the air currents in the room, etc., then the laws of physics should allow you to predict how it will land. If you think of randomness as being about our lack of knowledge of how things are going to turn out, then the coin flip seems random. If you think of randomness as being about some sort of indeterminacy in the world, independent of our knowledge, then the coin flip doesn't seem random. It's hard to know which is the better way to think of randomness.

Perhaps the best place to look for random events is quantum mechanics. Consider a single atom of a radioactive substance. Quantum mechanics allows us to compute the probability that the atom will decay in the next second. According to some interpretations of quantum mechanics, whether or not the atom will decay in the next second is not determined by the current state of the universe, so it is random not only in the sense that we can't predict it, but also in the sense that even if we knew everything there is to know about the atom now, we still couldn't predict it. (Contrast this with the coin example, where if we knew everything about the current state of the coin, we could predict the outcome of the flip.) It was Einstein's dissatisfaction with this kind of interpretation of quantum mechanics that led him to object that 'God does not play dice with the universe.' One alternative is so-called 'hidden variable' interpretations of quantum mechanics, in which there is additional information unknown to us ('hidden variables') that determines, in advance, whether or not the atom will decay. On this kind of interpretation of quantum mechanics, the decay of the atom is random only in the same sense that the coin flip is random – we can't predict it, but only because we lack some knowledge about the current state of affairs. Many people believe that hidden variable interpretations of quantum mechanics have been proven to be impossible, but there is, in fact, a successful hidden variables theory that was developed by the physicist David Bohm.

So is the decay of an atom random? The answer is that it may depend on how you interpret quantum mechanics, and it may also depend on how you interpret the word 'random'.

Q

66 *Science tells us that space is endless and ever expanding.*
But, if it's endless, how can it expand? And what is it
expanding in? 99

A

Daniel J. Velleman: When scientists say that space is
expanding, they don't mean that space has a boundary that
is moving outward – that would, indeed, be incompatible with
space being endless and therefore having no boundary. They
also don't mean that space is expanding 'in' something else –
some 'superspace' that contains space. All they mean is that
the distances between points in space are increasing. That can
happen even in a space that is endless, and it does not require
that the expansion take place in some larger space.

To understand this, it is helpful to distinguish between two
different approaches that mathematicians use to define geo-
metric properties of a space: the extrinsic approach and the
intrinsic approach. The extrinsic approach involves relating
the space to some larger space that it sits inside; the intrinsic
approach makes use of only the space itself, and not some
larger space that it sits inside.

For example, suppose we want to study the curvature of the
surface of the Earth. One way to see that the surface of the

Earth is curved is to image a flat plane tangent to the surface of the Earth at some point. We can detect and measure the curvature of the surface of the Earth by noting that the surface deviates from the tangent plane, and measuring the size of this deviation. But this deviation takes place within the three-dimensional space that the surface of the Earth is embedded in, so this is an extrinsic measure of the curvature. The curvature can also be detected by making measurements that take place entirely on the surface of the Earth. For example, if you lay out a large triangle on the surface of the Earth and measure the angles of the triangle, you will find that they add up to more than 180 degrees. This measurement makes no reference to a larger space containing the Earth's surface, so it is an intrinsic measure of the curvature of the surface.

Cosmologists use only the intrinsic approach when discussing the geometry of space. Thus, none of this discussion involves any reference to a larger space that space sits inside. Although they may use words that seem to suggest such a larger space, such as 'expansion' or 'curvature', those words are always being used to refer to some intrinsic property of space itself, and not some relationship between space and a larger space.

Q

66 *What happens to a moment of time after it occurs?* **99**

A

Mark Crimmins: Nothing happens to moments; things happen at them. After a moment passes, nothing that happens any more happens at it.

A past moment might, however, still be remembered and spoken of. Does that require that in some sense it 'still exists' and is indeed eternal? For surely there is *something* that we are remembering and speaking of. Or is that a mistake? Could it rather be that while there *was* something that we are remembering and speaking of, there *isn't* anything that we are remembering and speaking of? But is it coherent to say that in addition to all the things that there are, *there are* also things that there were but are no more? That sure sounds self-contradictory. How about: in addition to all the things that there are, *there are-or-were* also the things that were but are no more? Here, 'there are-or-were' functions as a 'quantifier' that covers things that no longer exist. Some philosophers hold that if you use a quantifier like that, you are committed to the view that the things it covers *do* exist (for there have to *be* the things it covers, for it to cover

53

them). Can we reply: No! there merely have to *be-or-have-been* those things? Is this disagreement resolvable? Is it substantive or merely a quibble about words?

Q

66 *Do philosophers have a better track record of making successful personal decisions than the average individual?* **99**

A

Richard Heck: In college, I had a professor who was both a devout Jew and a Kant scholar. Kant, you may know, was pretty anti-Semitic. I asked my professor how he handled that. He said to me, 'One wouldn't expect a geometer to be a triangle' – by which, I take it, he meant that someone who can think profoundly about moral questions need not be very good at putting theory into practice.

A

Jyl Gentzler: And why can't one expect someone with philosophical insight, like Kant, always to do the right thing?

Socrates assumed that once we knew what we should do, we would automatically act as we should. His student Plato disagreed – as have most philosophers since him. We have other sources of motivation besides knowledge of what is best. As Plato put it, we have certain appetites – whether natural or acquired – that are insensitive to considerations of what is best, and we have emotional responses that aren't perfectly calibrated to our view about what is best. For this reason, even if I believed that it would be a bad idea to give in to some temptation, I might still have appetites or emotions that overpower my better judgment. So, for example, I know that it would be a good idea to get more exercise. However unpleasant I find the atmosphere at the gym and however burdensome it is to take the time to bundle up properly so that I can manage the cold of a long walk in the winter, these immediate harms are quite obviously outweighed by the longer-term health, psychological, and aesthetic benefits of regular exercise. And yet, during the winter months, I just can't seem to motivate myself either to go to the gym or to take a brisk walk.

Q

&& *It has always struck me that philosophy is not a subject that has made any real progress. Why waste time constructing elaborate theories that are not scientifically provable? Why waste so much time pondering questions where (1) progress is hard to judge and (2) the resulting ideas do not really change the world in any significant manner?* **&&**

A

Richard Heck: It is a common complaint about philosophy that it never makes any progress. But this complaint, when not based upon a lack of information, seems to me to be based upon an unreasonably stringent conception of what would constitute progress.

I think it's pretty obvious that philosophy has made profound contributions to human knowledge and culture. John Locke's *Two Treatises on Civil Government*, for example, laid the foundation for the political system in the United States – Jefferson took parts of the *Declaration of Independence* from the second treatise, pretty much verbatim – and, despite the very real flaws of that system of government, its development was a good thing. But maybe you weren't thinking about moral philosophy. Well, René Descartes's *Meditations on First*

Philosophy helped to establish a conception of the world and what is required for knowledge of it that made it possible for empirical science as we know it to grow and flourish, and that was a pretty good thing, too. But maybe that isn't what you had in mind, either.

To speak for myself, I tend to think of philosophy (outside ethics) as what something is before it's science. Indeed, in Descartes's time, there wasn't any division between philosophy and science. There were just 'moral philosophy' and 'natural philosophy', and both the *Meditations* and Descartes's work on optics were part of what he would have called 'natural philosophy'. But it took thinking of the kind we would now call 'philosophical' for Descartes and others to achieve the understanding that allowed them to start doing the kind of work we'd now call 'physical science'.

This pattern has repeated itself throughout the last several centuries. Empirical psychology, as we know it, is little more than a century old. Its earliest practitioners – William James is one very good example – were philosophers as much as they were scientists. For the science of psychology to be born, much work had to be done trying to get a handle on what the problems were and how they could sensibly be approached before much could be done about actually approaching them. And one might well trace the origins of scientific psychology back through David Hume to Descartes.

In some parts of psychology today there is still much similar work to be done. That's especially true as regards work on consciousness.

This same kind of pattern repeated itself again when behaviourism was dethroned and replaced by cognitive psychology and the 'computer model of the mind'. Many of the leading figures in that episode would describe themselves as philosophers, though some of them might also describe themselves as psychologists or linguists. And, to be honest, I'm really not sure myself that a hard-and-fast distinction between philosophy and science is any more useful to us than it was to Descartes.

It's true that a lot of the old philosophical chestnuts are still unresolved: the mind-body problem, the problem of free will, and so forth. But I don't think it's true that no progress has been made on those problems, and it's certainly not true that we have made no progress understanding the nature of the mind. Progress has been slow, and it's not always easy to tell when progress has been made, but perhaps that's just because the problems are so hard. There has been enough progress over the last couple of centuries that empirical psychology is now a flourishing enterprise, and work by philosophers had a lot to do with that.

Q

66 Why can't philosophers agree?

In the natural sciences, you find disagreements at the frontiers of new research, but after some time has elapsed, agreement is reached and the frontiers advance to new areas of inquiry. In philosophy, nothing ceases to be controversial. What might progress in philosophy even look like? 99

A

Nicholas D. Smith: Philosophers don't all agree *because they won't listen to me*! Just kidding. In fact, I would really hate it if everyone's reactions to my views were: Oh, right. Well, that's it, then. That would be the *end* of philosophy, and I would not want to contribute to *that*!

There are lots of differences between what science does and what philosophy does, and one of these differences has to do with what I would call the domain of 'appropriate responses'. In science, the appropriate responses include (but are not entirely limited to): accepting the theory and the data offered in its support; holding the theory in suspense while one seeks to replicate (or fail to replicate) the data offered in its support; and rejecting the theory because one has some other data that are incompatible with the theory.

Much of what happens in philosophy (both where progress is made and where it is stalled) happens because we do not have access to the sort of data that clearly confirm or refute our theories. Our process is far less neat and far less orderly than that – we are still playing by the same rules the ancient philosopher Socrates worked with. One philosopher declares some theory, and then the rest of us, acting like Socrates, try to come up with reasons for thinking the theory is false, flawed or incomplete. In a way, then, the highest honour and attention one philosopher can give to another's work (though it doesn't always feel this way, mind you!) is to attempt to refute the other's work, because most philosophical attention is *critical* attention – someone devoting the time and intellectual resources to refuting my work is announcing to the world that he or she finds my work *important enough to merit such attention*, rather than best forgotten in silence. Best friends in the field are often one another's philosophical critics in the profession – and that is because we understand the *ethos* of philosophical activity, and philosophical progress: we kind of *back* into the future, by refuting present theories and then trying to figure out what that shows us for any future theoretical attempt.

So one reason philosophers never seem to agree is that *we're not supposed to agree*! Our *job* is to *disagree*, to a very substantial degree, because in that way we do our best to test whether the theories before us are true. If the best minds in the field can't find a way to disagree . . . well, then, maybe that would be The Final Answer. But whole careers in philosophy are made by coming up with new disagreements, and so we are very disinclined to agree with one another's theories – because by agreeing we are, in effect, acknowledging that we are not clever enough to have found whatever flaws might be there.

But this does not mean we do not make progress. There certainly are philosophical theories that have been given up for good (and for good reasons), and it is very plain that, thanks to our critical form of 'quality control', our theories now are a great deal more sophisticated (and less easily refuted) than those whose flaws we have studied and learned by heart in our training.

Part II

What Ought I To Do?

'It is very easy to point out some among our every-day judgments, with the truth of which Ethics is undoubtedly concerned. Whenever we say, "So and so is a good man," or "That fellow is a villain"; whenever we ask, "What ought I to do?" or "Is it wrong for me to do like this?"; whenever we hazard such remarks as "Temperance is a virtue and drunkenness a vice" – it is undoubtedly the business of Ethics to discuss such questions and such statements; to argue what is the true answer when we ask what it is right to do, and to give reasons for thinking that our statements about the character of persons or the morality of actions are true or false. In the vast majority of cases, where we make statements involving any of the terms "virtue", "vice", "duty", "right", "ought", "good", "bad", we are making ethical judgments; and if we wish to discuss their truth, we shall be discussing a point of Ethics.

So much as this is not disputed; but it falls very short of defining the province of Ethics. That province may indeed be defined as the whole truth about that which is at the same time common to all such judgments and peculiar to them. But we have still to ask the question: what is it that is thus common and peculiar? And this is a question to which very different answers have been given by ethical philosophers of acknowledged reputation, and none of them, perhaps, completely satisfactory.'

— G. E. Moore, *Principia Ethica*

Q

" Is it morally wrong to profit from other people's mistakes or stupidity? "

A

Thomas Pogge: Much depends on whether one is profiting passively or actively (taking advantage). *Passive profiting* is generally all right (as when you continue to enjoy the great view from your living-room because your neighbour mistakenly believes that it would be illegal to build a high-rise on the adjacent property). *Taking advantage* is generally wrong, especially when, exploiting another's stupidity, you cause her mistake (e.g., by provoking her to agree to an unwinnable bet). Somewhat less active cases are ones where you have no role in bringing about the mistake, but nonetheless do something to exploit it. This may be wrong – as when you pick up a chunk of money another has dropped and keep it rather than try to get it back to its owner. Or it may be all right in minor cases, as when you keep some change you find in a pay phone's coin return.

The moral situation changes in competitive game contexts in which such profiting is understood to be part of the game. In such a game (e.g., chess, poker, boxing), it is all right to trick your opponent into making a mistake and then to exploit this mistake as best you can. The same is true of the competition among firms or states. But there are three provisos: first, you may exploit your opponent's mistakes only insofar as the rules allow – you may not, for example, offer your chess opponent a sleeping pill that (you hope) he will mistake for a mint, or use your opponent's mistake in a wrestling match to choke him to death; second, your opponent's entry into the game must be voluntary and not itself a result of your luring her into the game by exploiting her stupidity (e.g., by suggesting that you are a very poor boxer or poker player when you are not); and third, the rules of the game must themselves be morally acceptable – taking advantage of another's mistake may not be justifiable in a competitive game context where the rules give you an unfair advantage from the start (or are otherwise morally unacceptable, as with duelling).

Q

66 *Was it ethical for Jews to evade taxes in Nazi Germany?* **99**

A

Oliver Leaman: It is an interesting question how far living in a state which persecutes a group of people justifies their retaliation by not obeying the law. Of course, as far as the practicalities of these things go, the choice to pay or not pay taxes is not much of a choice, since one has to pay them, and the consequences of not doing so were no doubt especially harsh in Nazi Germany. The Jews were of course particularly singled out through the tax system, especially if they wished to emigrate, and their assets were rapidly denuded through the legal system of the Third Reich. Might this not mean that they were morally allowed to break the law in situations where it was in their interests and possible to do so?

I think one has to be careful here. Many laws are just worth keeping because they make common life in the state bearable. Other laws, though, do not have this general character and might be regarded as only valid if they are part of a reasonably benign system. I was told by an elderly relative of mine who was himself a refugee from Nazi Germany that the socialists who fought with the police at demonstrations during the Weimar Republic debated long and hard among themselves whether when retreating from charging police officers they could run over lawns which bore notices forbidding access. Their point was that it was in everyone's interests for the grass to be healthy, and nothing the state could do would invalidate that fact.

This is perhaps the standard by which the tax question could be judged. Was it in everyone's interests in Germany for taxes to be paid? The answer is probably negative, and if the regime could have been weakened by non-payment then so much the better. I think in this case the moral exigencies of the case and our intuitions both pull in the same direction.

Q

66 *Are there any moral constants over time? Is there anything*
that all societies have rejected as immoral? For example,
we think slavery is wrong now, but other societies at
different times have had little problem with it. Is this
cultural relativism? 99

A

Jyl Gentzler: If you look around the world or study human
history, it is easy to be impressed by the apparent diversity of
moral opinion. Moreover, it might seem that certain moral
disagreements – e.g., concerning the morality of early-term
abortion – are not rationally resolvable. And this observation
can easily lead one to the conclusion that morality is simply a
matter of opinion. However, it seems to me that the evidence
for a significant degree of rationally irresolvable moral disagreement is not as great as it seems at first sight.

Let's take for example the moral principle that one should
never significantly harm another person just for the fun of it. I
have never heard of any society or culture in which this moral
principle is not accepted. Of course, in different societies there
will be disagreement about the circumstances in which it *is*
permissible to cause harm to another individual. Yet I think that
in many cases the basis of this disagreement is not disagreement

about value, but disagreement about how the world works – about how the gods might react to certain events, about whether certain valuable social institutions could survive in the face of socially deviant actions, about what sort of practices promote physical and psychological health, and so on.

Further, some apparent moral disagreement is simply the result of the fact that, in different circumstances, the same moral principles can have different practical implications. For example, today in the West, the practice of female infanticide would generally be deemed morally abhorrent. Yet in southern India, in a context in which living conditions for women are particularly harsh, some mothers reluctantly conclude that such a practice is morally required. Yet were we to look more closely at the basic moral principles that lie behind these different practices in different contexts, we might well discover that they are in fact the same.

Finally, some apparent moral disagreement is quite literally deceptive. 'I have a right not to share these toys,' the sophisticated Joey protests to his mother when she urges him to share his toys with his friends. 'They're mine.' While Joey and his mother might appear to be engaged in a significant moral disagreement about the extent of property rights, in fact they are not. Joey is motivated by a concern to protect his narrowly conceived self-interests. Yet even at his tender young age, Joey has learned that it is often expedient to disguise such motivations in the language of moral principle.

A

Joseph G. Moore: The cultural relativist holds that the moral status of a given action or practice – whether it's right, wrong, permissible, honourable, and so on – depends upon the moral code of the culture in which that action is performed. (There are many variations, but that captures the general idea.) People are attracted to cultural relativism because it seems to honour our sense that polygamy, for example, is not absolutely right or wrong: it can be wrong in one culture but perfectly acceptable in another, *and* neither culture is morally incorrect in its practice. My own view is that cultural relativism is neither good nor bad, but wildly implausible. On this at least, I'm with Pope Benedict XVI, who has recently inveighed against the 'dictatorship of relativism'.

I doubt that on reflection we really are cultural relativists. And this is the most significant strike against it. We confuse it for attitudes like humility and tolerance that we do endorse. Human sacrifice, infanticide, torture, slavery and socially sanctioned rape have been practised in many cultures. And though I might understand how such practices arose, and even why otherwise rational and sensitive people might have indulged in them, I nevertheless regard these practices and their practitioners as wrong – and wrong absolutely. My moral convictions are less certain about other matters – for example, trophy hunting, prostitution, arranged marriage and even abortion. For this reason, and also because autonomy is a very great good, I'm inclined to tolerate these practices (or even another culture's ban on them) despite my disapproval. But humility and tolerance are quite different from cultural relativism. In fact, we regard them as absolute goods, I think, and disapprove of people and societies that are morally arrogant or intolerant.

There are also vexed problems in applying cultural

relativism, for we need to know what counts as the relevant 'culture' and its moral code, and these are often unclear. My neighbours disagree sharply about the status of abortion. So is abortion right or wrong relative to the culture of Sunderland, Massachusetts? And do the citizens of Sunderland even count as my culture, or should I include the views of my family and friends who are scattered around the globe? The complications seem even more hopeless when we apply the view to actions performed in one culture that affect another, or those performed by a person from one culture within a different culture.

The real failing here isn't so much that cultural relativism is imprecisely formulated; rather that it's a view that settles moral matters in an implausible fashion: the cultural relativist treats morality as a local popularity contest, and not as a subject matter open to reason, and to considerations that go beyond mere opinion. Because of this, the view makes a hash of moral reform and moral argument. Consider a lone abolitionist living in a society that permits slavery. According to cultural relativism, the abolitionist is simply misguided in claiming that slavery is wrong, since the moral code of her culture clearly allows it. The arguments the abolitionist may have to support her view, no matter how compelling, are simply irrelevant. And when someone from a free state debates slavery with someone from a slave-holding state they don't disagree, according to the cultural relativist, so much as talk past one another: slavery is wrong relative to the first culture and permissible relative to the second. The arguments are so much window-dressing. But this gets things entirely backwards: a practice isn't wrong merely because we believe it to be wrong; rather we strive, with the help of reason and argument (and also sensitivity, empathy and knowledge of empirical considerations), to believe those things to be wrong that are, in fact, wrong – and to do so because they're wrong.

Q

“ *Despite what's commonly said, is there actually anything really wrong with being hypocritical?* **”**

A

Peter Lipton: Being hypocritical might mean that I argue for a standard of behaviour that I do not myself meet. Thus I might argue that all parents should send their children to public (state) schools, even though I send my children to a private school. My behaviour does not undermine whatever force my argument may have. But there is a sense in which I must be getting something wrong: either the claim I am arguing for or my behaviour. Still, I am not necessarily misrepresenting myself. If on the other hand, what you mean by 'being hypocritical' is that I misrepresent my own position, for example by saying that parents ought to send their children to public school when I don't believe that, then we have a different wrong: the wrong of dishonesty.

Q

66 *Is it morally wrong to tell children that Santa exists?*
Regardless of how much joy and excitement kids get from
believing the Santa myth, it is an outright lie! Should we
always take the moral high ground and tell the truth where
children are concerned, or should we make exceptions?
When they find out the truth, aren't we teaching children
that no one, not even their parents, can be trusted? 99

A

Mark Crimmins: This is an interesting question about which I have no settled view. I was relieved when our kid tricked the truth out of us early on.

Probably it's true that when a kid discovers the Great Santa Lie, their disposition to assume that their parents are always telling the complete, literal truth diminishes somewhat. But surely the big question of trust is not whether parents can be counted on always to tell the complete, literal truth, but whether they can be counted on to act in the kid's best interests. Intentionally misleading the child in a way they're sure to discover may normally undermine this trust (and so it does seem a bad idea in general), but I see no reason to assume that it always would. And indeed I think kids often react to their growing awareness that there's no magic, no Santa, and so on, not with resentment for being convinced otherwise but with a wistful attempt to keep up the charade just a while longer. So long as you are trustworthy in general and especially when it really matters, giving your kid a false belief that has very low costs and that produces, as you say, joy and excitement, might be just fine. I certainly don't harbour a grudge about it with my parents.

A

Louise Antony: I have a very strong opinion about this, one that puts me seriously at odds with some of my very best friends: I think that there are no good arguments for teaching a child to believe in Santa Claus, or for not telling the child the truth the first time he or she asks.

Prima facie, one shouldn't lie to one's children. More seriously, one has a duty not to try to positively convince them of things that are beyond false, that are preposterous. Now what is supposed to make inculcating belief in Santa Claus an exception to this prohibition? The fact that the child will experience joy while he or she believes it? That can't in general be an argument for inculcating preposterous beliefs, since there are many preposterous beliefs that would bring a person joy, were a person to believe them: the belief that he or she is the most intelligent person in the world, that he or she will live for ever, that there are no calories or cholesterol in *fettucine alfredo*. There are also risks for the believer in believing preposterous things, some of which Mark Crimmins notes. In the case of Santa Claus, the risk of losing trust in one's parents' testimony is, I think, not trivial. Finally, when a parent actively tries to get a child to disregard perfectly sound arguments against a certain proposition, there's the risk that rationality will itself becoming devalued, that the child will get the message that making sense is not terribly important. 'But does a *reindeer* fly?' 'It's *magic*!'

So it's not clear that the 'joy' children get from belief outweighs the likely negative results. But the clincher is that *children don't have to believe in Santa Claus* in order to experience the 'joy' the questioner refers to. Children can get enormous pleasure out of the *pretence* that there's a Santa Claus, just as they enjoy the pretence that there's a Big Bird or a Superman. What I strongly suspect is that it's not the *kids'* joy that's at stake – it's the *grown-ups'*. It's the parents who enjoy the fact that their kids are 'innocent' enough to believe anything they're told, or who enjoy observing the 'cute' things kids say and do when they believe something that the grown-ups know to be absurd. Grown-ups don't have the right to such pleasures, and should give them up.

No, Virginia, there is no Santa Claus. Good for you for figuring it out.

Q

66 *How do we know that what people say is morally right is actually right?* **99**

A

Nicholas D. Smith: Some moral judgments seem to be so obvious that no one seriously doubts them – for example, that it is wrong to set fire to infant human beings. But with the exception of such obvious cases, we generally don't *know* what is right and what is wrong – we have to use our judgment about this, and human judgment, as I suppose you already realise, can be very fallible and faulty. But just because we don't *know* something, it doesn't mean that we should just give up or not try – questions of right and wrong are really, really important ones, and so we need to try and do our best when we make these kinds of judgments.

The way we philosophers try to do our best is to consult with the main theories and explanations of right and wrong that very smart and thoughtful people have offered and then think about how those theories apply to the cases we have to judge.

So let me give you three different sorts of theories (and these are not the only ones, but they are commonly regarded as three of the main ones), just to give you an idea of how this works:

(1) *Consequentialism.* In a consequentialist view, you try to figure out what sorts of consequences are desirable, and what sorts are undesirable. Then, you consider what courses of action are available to you, and do your best to forecast all of the foreseeable results that are relevant to the desirable and undesirable outcomes. The best decision will be the one that seems most likely to bring about the better results, and least likely to bring about the worse results, taking everything you can foresee into account.

(2) *Deontology.* A deontological view is one that tries to understand rightness and wrongness by some basic rule that we would be prepared to adopt just in principle. So, for example, Immanuel Kant proposed what he called the 'categorical imperative'. One of the ways Kant formulated this imperative was: 'Act only on that maxim through which you can at the same time will that it should become a universal law.' In other words, your act will be moral just in case it is a kind of act that you would have everyone follow always.

(3) *Virtue theory.* In this view, you think about what a truly excellent human being would be like, and you try to model yourself after that person in how you act – and even, to the extent that you can, in the ways you think and feel.

These different theories, however, sometimes would lead you in different directions, and when they do, you are back to trying to use your own judgment as well as you possibly can, by trying to figure out all of the relevant issues at stake. So even if you do learn these theories very well . . . you still can't *know* that what you decide to do is right or wrong, in many cases. But we often have to act without really *knowing* what would be the best course of action. We can't always know what is going to happen when we go driving in a car, right? But some drivers are still good drivers (and some, not so good!), because they learn what they need to learn to handle a car, and then they drive alertly and cautiously at all times.

The same is true in judging right and wrong. Being alert to the alternatives and the relevant issues, cautious (don't think you *know* something when you don't!) and aware of your own limitations are all very good characteristics when one needs to make a moral judgment. And there is simply no avoiding the issue: we all do have to make such judgments a lot of the time. So the aim is to make them as well as we can, even when we aren't in a position to *know*.

Q

66 *Do luck and bad luck exist? Or have they just been imagined in order to create excuses?* **99**

A

Thomas Pogge: Some philosophers have held that good and bad luck does not really exist because the universe is deterministic (running like clockwork according to strict physical laws). I assume this is not your concern. You point out, quite rightly, that people appeal to bad luck as an excuse, and that such appeals are often implausible and put forward in bad faith. This is true. Nonetheless, we should not say that *all* such appeals are implausible. Surely there are some cases of genuine bad luck, cases where things really turned out worse than the agent could reasonably have predicted. Before the age of computers, the philosopher John Rawls once very nearly lost the only typescript of his masterpiece *A Theory of Justice* to an office fire that he could not possibly have foreseen. Had the script indeed been destroyed, this would have been a genuine case of bad luck – for him and for the rest of us. Recognising such genuine cases of bad luck does not prevent us from rejecting the lousy excuses you are rightly worried about: we can point out that the outcome was not really worse than the agent could have predicted or that the agent failed to take sufficient account of the risk. For example, we can tell the notorious drunk driver that it was *not* unpredictable that he would cause an accident sooner or later. Or we can tell him that, though he encountered a low-probability challenge and was in this regard unlucky, he is nonetheless not excused because he ought not to have run the risk of encountering such a challenge while driving drunk.

People sometimes excuse their general failure in life by saying that they are prone to bad luck. Now, it is true enough that, in retrospect, some people have better luck than others. If you roll billions of dice ten times each, it is *likely* that some of them will score a perfect 60 and some an abysmal 10. We should recognise this and excuse people who have had to deal with much more than the average burden of misfortunes. But the causal or explanatory claim suggested by the phrase 'prone to bad luck' is false. People have such a proneness no more than coins do. And so we should therefore reject this excuse: 'I am an unlucky person, everything I try to achieve goes wrong, so I won't even try any more.' We can respond to this by saying that whatever bad luck someone may have had in the past will not make them any more likely to have bad luck in the future.

Q

66 *Consider the following scenario: my mother wants me to visit her for Christmas, but I don't want to. Should I go out of duty?*

According to some philosophers, like Kant, good actions must be motivated by a sense of duty, as opposed to inclination. But shouldn't it be just the other way round, at least if the action is about doing another person a favour? It seems almost immoral to do somebody a favour only because of a sense of duty. 99

A

Matthew Silverstein: Kant never says that *good* actions must be motivated by a sense of duty. What he does say is that actions have *genuine moral worth* to the extent that they are performed out of a sense of duty. Many philosophers have certainly felt as you do – namely, that there is something backwards about this claim. I find it strangely compelling, and I'll try to explain why.

Kant actually provides a wonderful example in his great book, *Groundwork of the Metaphysics of Morals*. There he asks us to imagine someone (let's call him 'Joe') who spends his life doing good merely because he feels like it. He has a natural desire to help other people, and he takes great pleasure in meeting others' needs. Kant acknowledges that Joe's actions are 'right' and 'amiable', but he denies that these actions have any true moral worth. Kant believes that moral esteem is esteem of a very special sort. It is a sort of awe that we reserve for a select few actions and characters. But is there anything especially impressive or awe-inspiring about Joe simply doing what he wants to do – about Joe doing what feels good? Of course, we're glad that Joe happens to be the sort of person who takes pleasure in helping others, but given that that's the sort of person he is, there is nothing remarkable about his benevolent actions.

Now suppose that Joe becomes depressed – that his mind is 'overclouded by sorrows of his own which extinguish all sympathy with the fate of others'. And suppose that – despite his depression and the fact that he takes no pleasure in helping others – Joe continues to do good deeds, merely because he knows that it's the right thing to do. He no longer has any natural inclination to be benevolent: all of his desires seem to be urging him to stay in bed or watch TV. Nonetheless, through sheer force of will, Joe 'tears himself out of this deadly insensibility' and performs good deeds 'for the sake of duty alone'. Now *that's* impressive – even awe-inspiring. When Kant says that only actions done from duty have moral worth, he is simply suggesting that we reserve a special sort of praise or esteem for actions that are done in the face of opposing inclinations.

Note that the morally worthy version of Joe is not necessarily the version we'd want to have over for dinner. He actually sounds rather unpleasant. We'd much rather surround ourselves with people like the generous and good-spirited Joe who just enjoys helping others. Why, then, does

Kant think that only the actions of the other, depressed Joe are morally worthy? Perhaps because only *that* Joe – only the Joe with that kind of dedication to his duty – is guaranteed to do the right thing. Kant's worry may be that people who do good deeds because they feel like it will stop doing them when they stop feeling like it. If, on the other hand, you're doing something because you think it's the right thing to do, then it seems that you're likely to do it regardless of how you feel.

Let's now return to your example. Suppose you return home to visit your mother at Christmas not because you want to, but only because you think it's the right thing to do. It *does* seem that there is something unsavoury about you in this example, but it doesn't follow that you're acting immorally or that your action has no moral worth. What it lacks is *some other kind of worth or value*! In this example, you come off as unloving, ungrateful or unpleasant. (Of course it's only a hypothetical scenario. I'm sure that in reality you *love* visiting your mother!) As far as Kant is concerned, the fact that you don't want to see your mother only makes your action that much more impressive, at least morally speaking. After all, there's nothing especially noteworthy about a loving and devoted child returning home for Christmas. In a way, though, there *is* something noteworthy about an unloving and ungrateful child coming home for the holidays. And it's just that special something that Kant calls *moral worth*.

And so, for Kant, moral worth is actually something rather peculiar. The fact that someone is worthy of moral esteem doesn't in any way entail that they're worthy of other sorts of esteem. If you feel no inclination at all to visit the woman who changed your diapers, attended all of your soccer games, explained to the principal that the dog really did eat your homework, and in general has lovingly cared for you your entire life, then you may not be a naturally generous or amiable person. You may be downright mean! If you visit anyway – just because you know it's the right thing to do – then your action has moral worth. But this moral worth doesn't make you any more amiable or generous.

Q

66 *Should the tolerant tolerate intolerance?* **99**

A

Louise Antony: There is, as you suggest, something paradoxical about tolerance. But the air of paradox can be dispelled if we distinguish two different things that people can have in mind when they talk about 'tolerating' something. There is a sense of 'tolerate' that means 'is indifferent to', as in 'I don't see why those parents tolerate that kind of behaviour from their children.' This is the sense I think people intend when they say, plausibly, that no one should tolerate racism, sexism or, for that matter, intolerance.

But this isn't the sense in which 'tolerance' is a virtue. The kind of tolerance required for a civil society is the kind that acknowledges the rights of every person to make up her own mind and to form her own opinions, and that makes illegitimate any attempt to coerce anyone to change her mind. In this sense, there's no incompatibility between tolerating a racist belief, and trying, by all legitimate means of persuasion, to change the opinion of the person who holds it. It is in this sense that a tolerant person should 'tolerate' intolerance; she must acknowledge the right of someone to disagree with her about the value of tolerance, or about the right of others to hold particular opinions. But the tolerant person does not need to ignore or endorse intolerance, and can do her best to *argue* against it at every opportunity.

Q

&& Can a good deed offset a bad one, or does the moral worth of each exist independently? 99

A

Matthew Silverstein: Suppose that after receiving some particularly bad grades, John – a good-for-nothing graduate student – kills innocent Mary in a fit of rage. Aware of the terrible nature of his action, John spends the rest of his life trying to make up for his crime. After serving his time and 'paying his debt to society', John devotes himself to the goals that were most important to Mary. It turns out that she was a dedicated advocate of the preservation of endangered species, and thus – even though he has never really cared much about wildlife – John becomes just such an advocate himself. He donates large sums of money to the World Wildlife Fund and works as a volunteer as often as he can. In order to atone for his horrible crime, John commits himself to living a virtuous life and to seeing that at least some of Mary's life projects are fulfilled. John's commitment is so great that he almost single-handedly saves the wingless, spotted, nine-toed bat from extinction!

With this example in mind, let's return to your question. None of John's subsequent actions makes his initial crime any less wrong. No amount of repentance or benevolence can erase the wrongness of a murder. And so, to answer the second half of your question first, the moral worth of a particular action depends only on the action itself and the reasons for which it is performed. However, there is more to morality than the moral worth of individual actions. We also make moral judgments about *people*, and here a good deed *can* offset a bad one. When it comes to evaluations of a person's moral character, subsequent acts can and should play a role. Thus, our assessment of John's character – of *his* moral worth, rather than the moral worth of his action – surely is (and ought to be) affected by his bat-saving behaviour. Even though we will continue to condemn his killing of Mary, we may come to respect and even to admire his life dedicated to virtue and to the preservation of strange endangered species.

Q

66 *I have a friend who keeps a stack of $100 bills under her bed. For some strange reason, she does not ever wish to spend the money; she just plans on letting it sit there. What's more surprising is the fact that she never counts it. So she would never know if some went missing.*

Am I justified in taking a bit of the cash to, say, buy her flowers? She would be pleased to receive the gift, I'm sure; at the same time she would not have the slightest idea that the money used to pay for it was her own. So as far as she can tell she benefits, so it seems I'd be doing her a favour. Yet, isn't it obviously cruel of me even to consider duping her like that?

What is going on here? **99**

A

Jyl Gentzler: Initially, your case strikes me as an instance of a moral principle to which I am committed: if no harm is done, then no wrong is done. If no one is harmed by, say, dancing, then moral prohibitions against it are unjustifiable. If no one would be harmed by your buying your friend flowers with her own money, then it follows from this principle that there are no grounds for moral complaint against your doing so. If your friend doesn't plan to use the money and if she doesn't care enough about it to count it once in a while, it can easily seem that you should steal the money and buy the flowers. After all, she receives no clear benefit from the money, she doesn't plan to use the money for any other good purpose, and receiving flowers is always very nice.

However, I am not yet convinced that you should do it. I wouldn't say that it is 'obviously cruel' for you to dupe her. I would reserve the word 'cruel' for people who are completely indifferent to, or even take pleasure in, the suffering of others, and your stealing her money in order to buy her flowers doesn't reveal such a character trait. Nonetheless, it is not so clear to me that you do not harm your friend by buying her flowers with money that you steal from her and by pretending that the money that you spent was yours. The institution of private property – of giving individuals a large degree of control over certain items – offers clear benefits to owners (which in some circumstances might be outweighed by harm done to non-owners). Control over certain types of objects enhances the control that we have over our lives, and many people have held that such control is both intrinsically and instrumentally valuable for human beings. Even if your friend is not now planning to do anything with her money, her possessing this money gives her a certain amount of control over her life which she would not otherwise have. Apparently, she has no use for the money now, but she could easily develop new interests and, to serve these interests, a little extra cash might be handy. To take this control away from her is to harm her, whether or not she ever becomes aware of this harm. Further, the false belief that you spent some of your own very limited, hard-earned money in order to buy her flowers might lead her to think better of you than you in fact deserve. This misinformation might lead her to make decisions about her future relationship with you that she would not have made had she known that the money you spent was in fact hers. Your deceit would thus further erode the control that your friend has over her life, and thus harm her even more.

A more difficult question, it seems to me, is why you shouldn't steal her money in order to give money to Oxfam (or some other very worthy cause). Sure, you take away some of the control that she has over her life, but you potentially save lives.

Q

" Do the advances in the field of biotechnology threaten our moral values? "

A

Louise Antony: Developing technologies have always caused new ethical challenges to arise, often by making once impossible states of affairs possible. Insofar as our ethical thinking has failed to take account of these new possibilities, our ethical systems will be tested. But I see no reason to think that foundational ethical facts, like the wrongness of causing gratuitous pain to a sentient creature, are under any threat from new inventions.

You probably have in mind developments like *in vitro* fertilisation and cloning. These developments challenge us to think harder about what is really at the heart of moral personhood – is it the mere biological fact of being human, or is it rather certain morally important capacities, like being able to feel pain, or being able to reason? Technological advances such as these also raise questions about what human beings have the right to try to control, since they offer us the prospect of intentionally affecting things we had no control over at earlier times in our histories.

Notice that technological developments can also make it easier for us to follow our consciences. We now have the technological wherewithal to feed everyone in the world – all that's lacking is the will.

Q

66 I know I feel very strongly about the importance of conserving biodiversity, but I really can't pin down why it is so important to me, or how to convince others that it is important. Can philosophy help? 99

A

Joseph G. Moore: Philosophy can help us sift through and evaluate the possible reasons for conserving biological diversity – not just diversity of species, but also diversity of ecosystems, and perhaps even genetic diversity within a species. What's worrying about our current situation, by the way, is not simply that species are going extinct (this has always happened), but that they are doing so at an alarming rate and on an alarming scale – one that is comparable to the five or so mass extinctions that have taken place over the past 500 million years. And we seem to be causing it!

There are several very good instrumental reasons for preserving biodiversity. First, in biodiversity lies a treasure chest of unknown medicines, foods, and even industrial applications that may be of great use to us. Second, it holds clues to a better understanding of the Earth's biological history and workings. And third, for many of us, the diversity of life is a deep and awesome source of aesthetic, and even spiritual fulfilment. These are all instrumental and anthropocentric considerations because the value they give to biodiversity derives entirely from the benefits it brings to us, humans. For this reason, they don't support conservation at all costs: the survival and flourishing of humans may well outweigh the preservation of some rare tick, or leech, or bog of some peculiar kind whose benefit to us we might justifiably estimate to be minimal.

What's philosophically interesting is whether biodiversity also has any non-instrumental or intrinsic value: do species or ecosystems have interests or rights that we should respect independently of any benefit that doing so might bring to us? This question is different from the question of animal rights. We might well believe that the interests of individual non-human animals should be given moral weight – that we should abolish factory farming and animal experimentation, for example – without believing that there is some extra weight to be given to rare animals, or to life-forms that promote diversity, or to 'holistic' entities like species, biotic communities, entire ecosystems, or even Mother Earth considered as an integrated system (this is roughly the Gaia Hypothesis). Whether such entities have intrinsic value is really the central question in environmental philosophy, and it runs through a great variety of ancient and contemporary philosophical and religious traditions.

I've always wanted to believe that holistic entities have intrinsic value, but have never been able to. For one thing, notions of ecological stability and balance, of an ecosystem, and even of a species (not to mention the Gaia Hypothesis) are scientifically problematic. But even waiving this, I can't see a compelling reason why such entities would have intrinsic value of a type that should command our moral respect. That's why I fall back on the instrumental reasons in support of my broadly environmentalist inclinations, including my conviction that we should do much more to preserve biodiversity. But other, perhaps more visionary, people don't shy away from granting intrinsic value to these holistic entities.

Q

66 *Since life first evolved on Earth, a huge number of species
have developed only to become eventually extinct, a key
feature of Darwin's 'survival of the fittest' model of
evolution. Many species face extinction today – is it right
for mankind to intervene to try and stop this process?* 99

A

Mark Crimmins: Saying that natural selection favours the
'fittest' creatures makes it sound like interfering would
obviously be bad, because it would risk diminishing a good
thing, namely fitness.

But first of all, there is nothing in Darwin's explanation of
natural selection that assigns any value, positive or negative,
to reproductive fitness. The central idea, of course, is that
when genetically passed-on traits cause members of a species
to have more descendants than others, the traits become more
common. That has nothing at all to do with whether the
outcome is 'for the best' in any sense. It's just what will in fact
happen.

Second, the role of humans in a way changes nothing: we
are part of the environment, and our behaviour affects the
natural selection of other species fundamentally no differently from any other environmental factor. Our fondness for

juicy oranges or annoyance with intrusive coyotes can explain why certain organisms have more or fewer offspring than others in the same way that facts about climate and competing species can. Similarly for our preference, say, for biodiversity, or for slowing the rate of extinctions caused by others of our behaviours. 'Fitness' can just as easily be the capacity to thrive in a nature preserve as the capacity to survive in a sewage-thick bay. So our 'interference' can be seen, not as counteracting selection of the fittest, but as influencing which organisms, with which traits, will in fact exhibit fitness.

Still, to point out that the basic theory of natural selection has no consequences about what it would be right or wrong for us to do in influencing its course leaves completely open what considerations really do bear on the moral issue. Surely there are practical concerns – we might one day have use for many of the species that are dying out (and who knows which ones?); the effects of extinctions on ecosystems may be of serious practical concern for humans. Are there, in addition, more purely moral reasons to favour a conservative approach to our custodianship of the planet's biodiversity? Do we have duties to species or to ecosystems, or responsibilities to future generations to leave things not so impoverished from how we found them? Someone should ask a philosopher.

Q

66 *How immoral is it that, despite rising awareness over the past few decades of Earth's limited resources, we continue to pursue a growth-dependent economy and grossly materialistic lifestyles which are clearly unsustainable and which must have catastrophic consequences, if not for ourselves, probably for our own children and certainly for coming generations?*

Since we are all participating in the plundering and spoiling of our planet, with whom does responsibility lie? And does the fact that we are in 'collective denial' of the consequences in any way reduce or excuse our culpability? 99

A

Thomas Pogge: It is not quite right to say that we are all participating in the spoiling of our planet. While the 16 per cent of world population residing in the high-income countries live on around $30,000 annually on average, the bottom half of humankind live on less (often much less) than $1,300 annually at purchasing power parity (corresponding to roughly $300 at market exchange rates). The bottom half are consuming and burdening the environment, but not excessively so. Nearly all the harms the question highlights are produced by their wealthier compatriots in the poorer countries and (especially) by the populations of the high-income countries. This point heightens our responsibility. We are plundering our planet and also appropriating the spoils of this plunder so lopsidedly that half of the human population still lives in dire poverty, which exposes 850 million people to hunger and malnutrition (UNDP) and causes millions of deaths (including annually 10.6 million children under the age of five) from poverty-related causes (UNICEF).

Responsibility falls on political leaders of industrialised and industrialising countries. Though some governments are doing much better than others in restraining the contributions their corporations and citizens make to environmental degradation and the persistence of severe poverty, nearly all societies are contributing far too much to these harms. In reasonably free and democratic societies at least, responsibility for these contributions is shared by ordinary adult citizens who can organise themselves to change the legal rules and policies of their government and can also make personal efforts to mitigate the harms their society is contributing to. Here, greater responsibility falls on citizens who are more privileged and influential, and also on those who profit more from the injustice. They ought to make greater efforts at social reforms or mitigation of harms.

Collective denial may render some such citizens less blameworthy – those who really never had reason to doubt that the environment is in good shape and that globalisation is reducing poverty just as quickly as possible. But most adult citizens in the high-income countries and most affluent citizens in the industrialising countries do not fit this description. They have reason to think about the issue, and decide not to. Each of them bears some share of responsibility for the ongoing harms of global poverty as well as for the present and foreseeable harms of resource depletion and environmental degradation. Given the magnitude of the harms at stake, this responsibility is quite substantial.

Q

66 *At what point can the end ever justify the means?*

I am particularly interested in your response in the context of criminal justice. For example, is it ever acceptable for a police officer to perjure herself to ensure a conviction of a defendant she knows to be guilty? **99**

A

Jyl Gentzler: What else could justify the means other than the end? The question, though, is what end we should have in view.

In the case that you imagine, it seems that the relevant end is getting a guilty criminal in jail. Let's assume for the sake of this discussion that we have no reason to doubt that such an end would be a good thing. Let's assume that the person is truly guilty of a violent and unprovoked crime and that he's very likely to continue his life of violence if left unchecked. We then weigh the good end of preventing further violence against the bad means of lying and it looks like, on balance, the goodness of the end outweighs the badness of the means. Not only, it seems, are we permitted to lie; in fact, we're morally obligated to do so.

The problem with this line of reasoning is that it doesn't take into account all of the relevant ends. In this context, when we are considering the ends, we must also consider the ends of the entire criminal justice system – namely, to protect the interests of *all* citizens – not only the interests of victims or potential victims of crimes, but also the interests of the accused. It's very important to all of us that we have a system in place that minimises the chances of being wrongly accused and convicted for a crime. We need to feel confident that we ourselves will not be mistakenly convicted, that our friends and family will not be mistakenly convicted, and that the truly dangerous, rather than the mistakenly convicted, will be stopped. To achieve *this* end, we agree to put certain rules into place which constrain the ability of any one of us to make decisions on the basis of a short-term cost-benefit analysis. It seems that overall, and in the long run, we're more likely to learn who has committed what crime if all of the witnesses are speaking the truth rather than deciding on their own whether the wrongness of deceit is outweighed by the benefits gained from conviction. For this reason, we put a rule against perjury in place and we back up that rule with a threat of punishment. An interesting further question is whether it is ever rational for any of us to consider ourselves exceptions to rules that we ourselves endorse.

Q

" *What is the difference between a terrorist and a freedom fighter?* **"**

A

Alexander George: If a *terrorist* is someone who seeks to achieve his goals either by terrorising innocents or through the threat of such terror and a *freedom fighter* is someone who is engaged in a struggle to liberate a population from a tyrannical ruler, then some freedom fighters have been terrorists, some freedom fighters have not been terrorists, and some terrorists have not been freedom fighters. If 'terrorist' refers to someone who's adopted a particular *means* and 'freedom fighter' characterises someone on the basis of his *goals*, then it's only to be expected that such cross-classification will arise.

In contemporary public political discourse, these terms are used less to describe reality than to express one's political approbation or condemnation of it. To call someone a freedom fighter is to laud him, while to brand him a terrorist is to excoriate him. Obviously, it's appropriate to make such moral judgments, but when political discourse consists of nothing but such judgments, unaccompanied by any reasoned justification for them, then the overall degradation of such discourse is assured.

In addition, these definitions are quite coarse and so can't be expected to be useful in describing the complexities of real-world situations. They are also misleading in encouraging the thought that the technique of terrorising innocents is one that is primarily adopted by individuals or perhaps relatively small groups: arguably, the more notable instances of such misdeeds have been committed by governments. Political discourse would be healthier if the labels were dropped, if we ceased to view the vast, varied world through such narrow slits, and if we sought to describe matters directly, clearly and honestly.

Q

" *How do philosophers justify war, if they ever do?* "

A

Peter S. Fosl: What an important question! It's difficult to be alive today and not reflect on this issue, isn't it? Anyway, you should be aware that some philosophers don't justify war. They hold that all war is immoral, either murder or something akin to murder. I am sympathetic with this view and believe that minimising or ending war is a goal we are obligated to pursue. But until we get there, I recognise the importance of developing what philosophers call 'just war theory'. In just war theory, philosophers distinguish between questions about when it is proper to engage in war (questions '*ad bellum*') and questions concerned with the conduct of the war ('*in bello*') once engaged. As you suggest, ideas about both of these are ancient and may be found in the Graeco-Roman, Abrahamic and Asian traditions. Typically, however, historians of philosophy turn to Augustine of Hippo (354–430) as the philosopher who initially formalised the theory. In the early modern era, other philosophers articulated an important theory of sovereignty, maintaining that nations should be free from external assault and remain free in the conduct of their internal affairs. More recently philosophers have explored the question of when sovereignty might be over-ridden in launching just wars; they have also worked to incorporate concepts of human rights into theories about the conduct of war. Dealing with issues of rebellion, resistance and terror has of course become acutely important. In any case, as I see it, the most important principles of just war theory today may be summarised as follows:

1. LAST RESORT: A just war can only be waged as a last resort. Reasonable efforts must be made to exhaust non-violent alternative ways to achieve the relevant objectives before the use of force can be justified.

2. LEGITIMATE AUTHORITY: Except where the government is incompetent or where armed revolution is warranted, a war is just only when a legitimate authority wages it.

3. JUST CAUSE: A just war can only be fought for a just cause. Here are four types of just cause:

    3a. *Wars of 'self-defence'*: Commonly, a just cause entails redressing a wrong already suffered. This principle, however, has been weakened in the following ways:

    3b. *'Pre-emptive' war*: Pre-emptive action may be launched in the face of an 'imminent threat'. This sort of threat must be an urgent, overriding, extreme necessity, where pausing for deliberation is unreasonable.

    3c. *'Preventive' war*: Currently illegal and easily a slippery slope, some argue for preventive attack even when danger isn't clear or imminent because contemporary threats are often clandestine and involve weapons of mass destruction.

    3d. *'Human rights interventions'*: Military actions are justified when the government of that nation either (1) violates on a large scale the human rights of those it rules or (2) is unable to protect those it rules from human rights violations committed by some third party (e.g., extra-state militias).

4. RIGHT INTENTIONS: A just war can only be fought with 'right' intentions. Material gain, revenge and the joy of conquest are not proper intentions. Halting a genocide is a proper one.

5. SUCCESS: A war can only be just if it is fought with a reasonable chance of success.

6. JUST GOAL: The ultimate goal of a just war is peace, not ongoing warfare.

7. PROPORTIONALITY: The force used in the war must be proportional, or on the appropriate scale, to the injury suffered. Participants are prohibited from using excessive or unnecessary force to attain the legitimate objectives of the war.

8. MINIMAL CASUALTIES: Military objectives in a just war should be achieved with a minimum of casualties, both combatant and civilian.

9. RIGHT MEANS: Weapons that are 'indiscriminate' in their destructive force, that kill on a mass scale, or that cause undue suffering are not permissible.

10. CIVILIANS: Civilians must be treated justly in the conduct of the war.

    10a. *Targeting*: The targeting of weapons used in war must discriminate between combatants and non-combatants.

    10b. *Collective punishment*: Punishments should be limited to those directly responsible.

    10c. *'Enemy combatants'*: Civilians should not be enlisted in military operations. Civilians who are directly involved in hostile military-like activities may be treated differently from other civilians but must at least receive the same protections afforded military prisoners, arguably more.

10d. *Occupation*: Occupying powers are responsible for the wellbeing of those living in territory they occupy.

11. PRISONERS: Prisoners must be treated humanely – not abused, tortured, starved or denied medical care, and not used to support the war effort.

12. OTHER TARGETING EXCLUSIONS: Sacred sites, cemeteries, historical and cultural artifacts should be spared. Adverse impacts upon natural habitats and populations of non-human plant and animal life should be minimised.

Q

66 *What justifies so many people, especially nasty people who don't show us any respect, in insisting on their 'human rights'? I mean, doesn't it need to be in my interest to respect bad people's rights?* 99

A

Thomas Pogge: Human rights are understood as very basic rights that every human being has. By virtue of having these rights, every human being enjoys some minimal moral protections against being treated in certain ways by other (individual or collective) human agents. And by virtue of having these rights, every human being also enjoys some minimal moral protections against having certain laws or social practices imposed upon him or her. For example, your human right not to be tortured imposes a stringent moral duty on all human agents that they not torture you and that they not collaborate in imposing upon you laws or social practices under which you are avoidably exposed to torture. Your human right to freedom of expression imposes a stringent moral duty on all human agents that they not prevent you from expressing yourself and that they not collaborate in imposing upon you laws or social practices under which you might well be so prevented. And your human right to basic necessities imposes a stringent moral duty on all human agents that they not deprive you of such necessities and that they not collaborate in imposing upon you laws or social practices under which you might well end up so deprived.

Now, your idea is that bad (nasty) people should be exempted from human rights. I don't think this is a good idea, for the following reasons. First, there is no agreement about exactly which people are bad. Take some group of which you are a member and then write down all members' names in two columns: good and bad. Let other group members do the same. I think you will find that the listings do not coincide. Very few of those you listed as bad will so list themselves. And some members may even list *you* among the bad – perhaps on the ground that you don't show them any respect. What should we do in the face of such disagreement? One plausible solution is to agree to respect the human rights of all, even those one thinks are bad, on the understanding that all others also respect the human rights of all (including those they deem bad). This solution shows how respecting the human rights of people you deem bad can be in your interest. This is in your interest insofar as it is part of a universal convention under which your human rights are respected even by those who deem you to be bad.

You may say in response that some people really are bad – they are not disposed to honour any universal convention of respecting human rights, and instead commit rape, mayhem or murder, for example. And, you will add, surely such people should be punished severely. Yes, indeed. By ascribing human rights to people, one is not protecting them from such punishment; one is merely making sure that such punishments are deserved. No one should be severely punished without a fair trial in which he can, with the help of a competent attorney, respond to the charges laid against him. The conduct he is accused of must have been criminal under a justified law at the time he engaged in it. And the evidence presented against him must convince an impartial judge or jury, beyond a reasonable doubt, that the accused is really guilty as charged. If, and *only* if, these conditions are satisfied may a severe punishment be inflicted on a person without violating this person's human rights.

You will notice that I am arguing here not merely against you, but also against the US and UK governments, which have in effect decided to follow your idea and not to respect the human rights of people they deem bad. As a result, thousands of people have been tortured and thousands are languishing in (often secret) jails – not only in Iraq, Afghanistan and Guantánamo Bay, but also in Jordan, Pakistan, Qatar, Thailand, Uzbekistan, other locations in Eastern Europe, and on the British island of Diego Garcia – with very little hope of ever being charged with any crime, ever having access to a lawyer, ever being able to communicate to their families that they are still alive. To find out what is known about these people, you can look at the research done by Human Rights Watch and Amnesty International.

Earlier I wrote that it is in your interest to respect the human rights even of those you deem bad insofar as such respect is part of a universal convention under which your human rights are respected even by those who deem you to be bad. Addressed to the US and UK governments, this appeal has much less force. They may well believe that they are powerful enough not to need the benefits of this convention. Still, even the most powerful agents have *moral* reasons to respect the human rights of all. One such reason, implicit in what was said before, is that many of those we deem bad may not actually be bad. As the research done by Human Rights Watch and Amnesty International shows time and again, many who have been detained for years as 'enemy combatants' are entirely innocent of any crime (and often not released precisely because they are innocent – it is much less embarrassing for the US and UK governments never to let such people resurface again than to make them reappear after years of abuse with mutually corroborating inside stories about secret detention facilities, the very existence of which is officially denied).

There are two additional moral reasons for respecting the rights of all others. First, even genuinely bad people sometimes become good or at least better. The prospects of this happening are generally brighter if we treat them with justice and humanity than if we give up on them by treating them like animals or monsters. Second, by treating evidently bad people without justice, we are also dehumanising ourselves. Toward the end of the Second World War, Churchill advocated that, once the war was won, the top Nazi leaders should be summarily shot like dangerous beasts. These Nazi leaders were among the worst people the world had ever seen and they had committed their crimes in such a public manner that there could be little doubt about their guilt. And yet, Roosevelt successfully insisted that they should receive a proper trial. Even if we did not owe it to them, we still owed it to ourselves and to their victims and to posterity to uphold in our treatment of them the very moral standards they had sought to obliterate once and for all.

This brings me to a last point. I agree with you that it is

hypocritical, if not grotesque, for certain very bad people to appeal to their human rights – bad people like Saddam Hussein or Suharto or Pinochet who, when they were in power, did not show the slightest concern for the human rights of those they killed and tortured. You can laugh at their appeals with contempt and nonetheless recognise the important moral reason (stated in the preceding paragraph) for giving them a fair trial.

Q

66 *What is the relation between law and morality? Do they always go hand in hand, or can there be immoral laws or illegal morality?* 99

A

Peter Lipton: Racist laws and laws concerning slaves provide examples of how legality and morality come apart. A law could make it legal to keep slaves, even if that is immoral; a law could prohibit one from helping someone of another race, even if that is morally obligatory. You can fail to do what is right without breaking any law, and breaking a law may not be immoral.

Q

66 Is it better to have a criminal justice system that runs the risk of freeing someone who will go on to commit a terrible crime, or one that runs the risk of convicting someone who is innocent? 99

A

Thomas Pogge: Any realistic criminal justice system will make both types of error: T-errors (terrible future crime committed by one wrongly acquitted) and I-errors (innocent person wrongly convicted). So, in designing our criminal justice system, should we give greater weight to avoiding T-errors or to avoiding I-errors?

There is a widely held view bearing on this question. One famous formulation by William Blackstone states: 'It is better that *ten guilty* persons escape than one *innocent* suffer.' I think what stands behind this view is the idea that we as a society bear a far weightier responsibility for harms to innocents that we directly bring about than for harms to innocents that we merely might have prevented. This idea is familiar in pedestrian contexts. It would be wrong to kill one innocent person in order to save another. It would be wrong to harm one innocent person in order to rescue another from a similar harm. It would be wrong to risk the life of one innocent person to prevent a risk to the life of another (risks being equal). And, it would be wrong to cause a risk of harm to one innocent person in order to prevent the same risk of harm to another. In all these cases, agents ought to give more weight to harms and risks of harm they directly bring about than to similar harms or risks of harm that they merely fail to prevent.

This almost answers the question you posed: we should give greater weight to avoiding I-errors than to avoiding T-errors. I say 'almost', because the average harm associated with errors of each kind may not be equal. So, the conclusion might conceivably be overturned if the average harm done by I-errors is just a few days in jail without public stigma while the average harm resulting from T-errors is a minor massacre. But, this is not true in the real world. Here, in order seriously to reduce the number of terrible crimes committed by persons wrongly acquitted, we would have to make it easier to convict people accused of very serious crimes and then take those convicted out of circulation for very long periods or forever. And doing this will inevitably increase the number of innocent people who, wrongly convicted, are locked up for very long periods or even executed.

Q

66 *The recent controversy surrounding the publication in a Danish newspaper of cartoons lampooning the Prophet Muhammad has given rise to claims that Danes and others should break taboos, and that freedom of the press and free speech are of a greater value than maintaining such taboos. Could the same claim be made around dialogue concerning the Jews and Nazi Germany?* **99**

A

Thomas Pogge: Yes, it makes sense to see these two cases as parallel. But I would not agree that Danes and others should break taboos. You are right that freedom of the press and free speech are of greater value than maintaining such taboos. Our countries should indeed outlaw neither cartoons that insult the prophet of Islam nor works that glorify the Nazis or deny the holocaust. But this claim is distinct from the first claim you identify, namely that citizens of our countries should break the relevant taboos. I do not think that people ought to glorify the Nazis, ought to deny the holocaust, or ought to publish cartoons that insult revered figures of other religions. In fact, I think they ought to refrain from doing such things (though, to repeat, doing them should be legally permissible).

We might then distinguish four classes of expressions: (1) those that ought to be outlawed and are morally wrong; (2) those that ought to be legal and are morally wrong; (3) those that ought to be legal and are morally indifferent; and (4) those that ought to be legal and are morally called for. In response to your question, we should think especially about class (2) to appreciate that there may be important reasons (e.g., respect for truth or respect for people of other faiths) to refrain from certain expressions that should nonetheless remain legal.

There are two strong reasons for defining freedom of speech and freedom of the press quite broadly, so that all or most morally wrong expressions are legally protected. The first reason is that the political process (the government) is generally unreliable at distinguishing morally permissible and morally impermissible expressions. If authorised to draw such a distinction, a government would often outlaw far too much – for example, all sorts of expressions that are critical of or embarrassing to itself. The experience of many countries, past and present, shows governments to have this tendency. It may well be better, then, not to give governments such authority and constitutionally to protect citizens' freedom to express themselves in ways that are morally offensive. The second reason is that outlawing the expression of certain views is often counterproductive. When a government uses the criminal law to suppress some opinion, many citizens may conclude that the government is afraid of this opinion and unable to refute it. And the suppressed opinion may then find more support among citizens than it would receive if it could be openly debated. This has in fact happened, I believe, with glorifications of the Nazis and denials of the holocaust. Such morally offensive views are most effectively marginalised not by legal prohibition, but by exposing them to free and open debate. (David Irving has apparently changed his mind about the holocaust on the basis of such responses from historians and others.) And the most effective response to the editors of that Danish newspaper may be a vigorous debate about why they declined to print the earlier cartoons insulting Jesus Christ.

Q

*66 Can cardiac resuscitation of an individual with an
inoperable brain tumour be justified? Who benefits? 99*

A

Peter S. Fosl: An interesting question, and one related, I
think, to the question of whether medical care should be
provided to those sentenced to death. As I see it, there are six
considerations that together justify the practice of resuscitating those dying of terminal illness who suffer cardiac arrest.
They are considerations rooted in the very nature of death and
dying – its variability, its inevitability – and the importance of
human dignity and autonomy.

1. *Universal mortality*: In a sense, we're all sentenced to
   death, as all of us are going to die at some point. You
   might say that those with inoperable brain tumours just
   have a clearer picture than most about when and how
   they'll die. Given the fact of universal mortality, knowing
   when and how one's going to die doesn't seem by itself to
   be a good reason to deny that person medical care.
2. *Probability, not necessity*: Notice, in addition, that even for
   those with inoperable deadly tumours the picture isn't
   perfectly clear. Typically, people face some probability

of death from the tumour, not certainty. Even one thousandth of one per cent chance of recovery is a chance and therefore a reason to administer resuscitation. Spontaneous remissions are not unknown.

3. *Time*: Even if death from the tumour were certain, a tumour takes time to kill. That time to live is likely to provide grounds for resuscitation. One of my uncles died of a brain tumour. While it was killing him, he spent his time visiting family and friends, getting his financial and legal affairs in order, making plans for the care of his spouse and child, attending religious services, listening to music, reading, travelling, etc. Had he suffered a cardiac arrest during that period and been refused resuscitation, he would have been denied this time well spent.

4. *Autonomy*: Deciding how to greet one's demise is a terribly important element of human self-determination. It seems meaningful to assist those who wish, as it were, to go down fighting.

5. *Rebellion*: The existentialist Albert Camus argued, persuasively in my opinion, that perhaps the central way of rendering life meaningful is to rebel or struggle against death, not to accept with acquiescence the ultimately crushing and annihilating reality of human existence. A story I once heard about the French artist Renoir seems to illustrate the sense of Camus's claim. It became at some point impossible for the ageing artist to hold his paintbrush any longer. So, in defiance of his degeneration, Renoir asked his assistant to attach the brush to his arthritic hand. Refusing Renoir's request and telling him that he would be dead soon anyway would have been to capitulate to meaningless annihilation and to rebuke his

choice about how to face it. She took the time and effort to tie the paintbrush to his hand, and in doing so she did the right thing.

6. *Resource availability*: Now, if (a) administering resuscitation required a social cost that seriously harmed those without tumours and if (b) death from the tumour were almost certainly imminent, then there would be grounds for refusing a resuscitation. Of course, there are situations where medical resources are scarce (e.g. in impoverished societies, war zones) and where resuscitating one patient would mean denying others. But in most cases the costs of resuscitation are low and resources remain abundant enough to provide for other people. In short, the availability of resources generally makes it possible to resuscitate terminally ill patients who have cardiac arrests without denying significant goods to others.

Of course, the autonomy of those who do not wish to receive resuscitation (especially those who have given advance directives to that effect) should also be respected. Otherwise, the uncertain, variable and often gradual process of dying in conjunction with considerations of universal mortality, autonomy, dignity and available resources lead clearly, I think, to the conclusion that generally we are all better off providing resuscitation to those with terminal illnesses, including inoperable brain tumours.

Q

❝ *I am a physician taking care of a woman with bad asthma who requires admission to the hospital. She happens to be six months pregnant, which is clinically relevant because low oxygen levels in the blood will affect the foetus. I inform her that if she refuses treatment, her unborn child will suffer oxygen deprivation and will likely be mentally retarded. She replied: 'God will take care of us, I'm going home.'*

Is my patient doing something morally wrong? If so, should I try to stop her? **❞**

A

Jyl Gentzler: To simplify the already complex moral issues at stake in this case, I'll simply assume that your patient is mistaken about God's intentions: God won't prevent harm to her foetus, nor will he offer any compensating benefits.

The answer to your first question is complicated by two facts: (a) the individual who would be harmed by your patient's lack of treatment is currently a foetus, and (b) your patient is apparently ignorant of the fact that she really is putting her future child at risk of harm.

While the rights of children are fairly uncontroversial, the rights of foetuses are highly contested. However, we can avoid this controversy by talking simply about your patient's future child. If this future child were to be mentally handi-capped because your patient now refuses to be treated, then her refusal of treatment would have made him much worse off than he would have been had she accepted treatment. Since your patient does not claim that she or anyone else would suffer significant harm if she were to *accept* treatment, I would conclude that your patient's refusal of treatment is morally wrong.

But doesn't it matter for the purposes of moral assessment that your patient sincerely believes that she is acting in the best interests of her child? The answer to this question depends on the object of our moral assessment.

An action can be wrong, perhaps because it has terrible consequences. Yet the person who does the wrong action might nonetheless be a good person because she intended to help others and she could not have reasonably anticipated the bad consequences of her action. To use a familiar example, a Good Samaritan might go to some trouble to save the life of a person who turns out to be a serial killer. Was the Good Samaritan's action, in this situation, morally correct? I would want to say 'no'. Had she not so acted, many valuable lives would not been shortened. No action with such bad (even if indirect) consequences could be morally right. Were she to face the choice again, knowing what she now does about the serial killer, the Good Samaritan (because she is good) would not make the same choice. Nonetheless, she could not be morally blamed for doing what she did because she had no way of anticipating the bad consequences of her actions. Let's return now to your patient. For the reasons that I offered above, I would say that her refusal of treatment is morally wrong. However, I would say that she's a bad person and morally blameworthy *only* if her ignorance of the likely harmful consequences of her action is itself blameworthy.

Second question: what are your moral obligations? On the assumption that your patient's behaviour is morally wrong, what follows? Unfortunately, not much. The fact that one person's potential actions are immoral does not by itself imply that another person is morally permitted to prevent her from acting immorally. Physicians play an important beneficial role within our society, and their ability to play that beneficial role could be jeopardised if they were to take it upon themselves (especially as a matter of professional obligation) to prevent their patients from acting immorally. Patients might refuse to get further treatment from those whom they regard as meddling doctors, and the health consequences for both patients and foetuses (and the future children they become) could be devastating.

Q

66 *I'm a medical doctor. I have had to do CPR (Cardio-Pulmonary Resuscitation) in public, outside of the hospital, at least six times in my life. Only once did a patient recover partly – for another two months. It is a well-known medical fact that a very small percentage of 'resuscitated' subjects recover entirely after their heart attack. If she survives, the patient will often be reduced to a vegetative state. I myself would definitely not want to be administered CPR in case of a heart attack.*

How does my behaviour/attitude square with the Golden Rule of doing unto others as I would have them do to me? I'm Dutch, and in Holland all medical doctors are sworn in with the Hippocratic Oath, which clearly conflicts with not administering CPR. Should I stop extramural CPR, or honour my oath in spite of my better judgment? **99**

A

Thomas Pogge: You would not want to have CPR administered to yourself. And you would also not want to be treated contrary to your wishes. In order to apply the Golden Rule, we need to know which of these two desires is controlling. I would think it is the latter. If so, you should administer CPR to those who would want to have CPR administered – thereby treating them in accordance with their wishes, just as you want to be treated in accordance with your wishes.

To be sure, what a heart attack victim wants or would want is often unknown. But we can overcome this ignorance by making available some simple cards or stickers through which people can communicate their choices ('please do/do not administer CPR in the event of a heart attack'). Still, many heart attack victims have no such information on them, and this problem cannot be wholly avoided. Doctors must therefore sometimes act under uncertainty. Here, I think, the burden of decision-making should not fall upon them. Society should give clear legal instruction to doctors about the 'default': about how doctors should act in the absence of special instructions from the patient. Such a default instruction is legitimate so long as each person is free to override it through an explicit personal instruction valid for himself or herself.

What if the state has not laid down any default instruction and no instruction can be found on the heart attack victim? Here I think you ought to administer CPR, simply because afterwards the patient has ways to end her life if she disagrees with your decision. By contrast, if you fail to administer CPR, contrary to what the patient actually would have wanted, the effect of your decision (her death) is final and beyond correction.

Q

66 *Suppose that I'm working on a medical treatment for a project with no known cure or even treatment. My subjects report that they feel much better after receiving the treatment, but subsequent study shows that the treatment is, in fact, ineffective and all that I'm seeing is the placebo effect.*

Can I ethically tell them the truth and thereby make them feel worse subjectively? Would that violate the 'do no harm' principle of medical ethics? 99

A

Jyl Gentzler: The injunction 'Do no harm' is hard to follow unless one knows what counts as harm, and there is no clear consensus about this issue.

It does seem that by making a person feel worse, I am harming her. Feeling bad is in itself a bad thing, and it might also lead to other bad things. If I feel bad, then I may not be able to do other things that I would otherwise enjoy, things that I might believe have value in themselves. As you suggest, such considerations might seem to count against revealing the truth to your patient. At the same time, in certain circumstances, I could be made to feel worse if I am prevented from learning the truth about my situation. If I have false beliefs, I might make choices that I would otherwise not make, choices that lead me to feel worse than I would otherwise have felt.

Could I be harmed *simply* by being led to believe something false about myself even if this false belief never leads to any decrease of good feelings or any increase in feelings of pain, dissatisfaction or discontent? Let's imagine that I believe about myself that I am widely admired and deeply loved by my friends and family and that this belief gives me deep feelings of contentment and satisfaction. But let's imagine also that I am completely deluded: I am ridiculed behind my back and privately despised by my friends and family. Let's suppose further that their secret is safe, unless you tell me the truth. Would I be made better off simply by learning the truth about my situation? Philosophers disagree about whether self-knowledge is itself of significant value, independently of the good feelings that it generally, though not always, makes possible.

In any case, most of us value knowing the truth about our situation, primarily because we believe that with such knowledge we can make better decisions than we could have made in ignorance, and better decisions than anyone else could have made for us. And even if we were somehow convinced that others could make much better decisions for us than we could make for ourselves and that we would feel much better if we were kept in the dark, most of us would *still* prefer to make our own imperfect (but informed) decisions. For these reasons, most philosophers have maintained that physicians should always disclose to their patients information about their medical condition (including, it would seem, what effect a given drug or placebo is having on their health).

Q

66 *Can someone's quality of life ever be so bad that you are justified in taking care of them against their will in order to improve it? If so, how bad does it have to be?* 99

A

Thomas Pogge: It all depends on the mental competence of the other person. If he's not very competent (a child, perhaps, or mentally disabled), then we may interfere with him even to prevent minor harms. One should never interfere with the freedom of fully competent adults in order to improve their quality of life. Still, when a person's quality of life becomes very low, her mental competence may come into question. It is very hard to think rationally when one is in severe pain, for example. And in such cases it may be justified, then, to take care of someone against her own will.

Here we still face the question of *who* is so justified. A good candidate is a family member who intimately knows the person and what she would wish if she were feeling better. A poor candidate is some stranger, driven perhaps by moral or religious values that the person does not share.

So, when a normally competent adult is in such bad shape that his capacity for decision-making is impaired, then others who know him well may interfere with his freedom in order to improve his quality of life in ways that (they sincerely believe) he would approve of were he fully competent.

Q

I never understood the bumper sticker 'Against Abortion? Don't Have One.' I mean, people who are against abortion believe that it is equivalent to, or close to, the murder of babies. But surely those who put this bumper sticker on their cars wouldn't favour a bumper sticker that suggested that if you're against infanticide, then the proper response is simply to refrain from killing babies. If it's murder, then shouldn't it be outlawed?

A

Thomas Pogge: Agreed, the bumper sticker has very little persuasive appeal to those it purports to be addressing. But something could be said against your more general point, as follows.

Suppose someone believes that abortion is morally (roughly) on a par with infanticide and murder, and also that infanticide and murder are terrible crimes that ought to be criminalised and punished severely. Would it be incoherent for such a person also to hold that the criminal law should not interfere with any woman's decision about whether to have an abortion or not?

One could hold these two views together – in fact, Mario Cuomo held them together when he was governor of New

York State. One could rationalise the combination like this: 'I am convinced that abortion is murder. But the grounds of my conviction are rooted in a religion that many of my fellow citizens do not share. In fact, my country is deeply divided on the issue of abortion, with many reasonable persons on either side. Under such circumstances, it would be wrong to use the criminal law to suppress conduct that many reasonable people conscientiously believe to be morally permissible. It is not wrong, by contrast, to use the criminal law to suppress infanticide and murder, because their status as terrible crimes is widely recognised by citizens from all the diverse walks of life.'

Although hard to fit on a bumper sticker, this point is nonetheless worth a thought. A pro-choice person can fully respect others' conviction that abortion is murder, yet still make a reasoned appeal to these pro-life people that they should not use their political power to make the criminal law conform to their largely religious convictions.

Q

❝ *I was born in the early sixties. When my mother got pregnant, my parents were unmarried, but they got married and I was born eight months later. On the whole, I've had a wonderful life and I'm so grateful that I had a chance to experience it. I can't help thinking that if my mother had had an abortion, she would have done a terrible thing to me. She would have cut my life short – so short, in fact, that I wouldn't have ever had a chance to experience anything at all! If murder is bad because it denies a good life to a person in the future, then isn't abortion even worse?* **❞**

A

Jyl Gentzler: If your mother had had an abortion at that time, then yes, alas, there would have been no you. However, it's also likely that, if your mother had done *anything* different on that fateful night in the early sixties – had she decided to stay home, had her date with your father been delayed by even a slight change in the traffic patterns – there would have been no you: that particular egg and that particular sperm just wouldn't have gotten together. In fact, had any of a multiplicity of other events in the past been different (e.g., had the weather been slightly different on that evening millions of years ago when your ancient ancestors got together), then there would have been no you. When you think of all of the events that had to conspire from the beginning of time to produce you, then it becomes clear how very lucky each of us is even to have lived for just one minute. The odds against us were astronomically high.

Now let's imagine all the many possible unions of human egg and sperm that might have developed into people who had a life as good as yours. For example, if your parents' date had started just a bit later, then someone else might have been conceived that night. Was your good fortune his loss? Should we feel sorry for him? Should we grieve the lost lives of all of the indefinitely many people who might have been, had things turned out just a bit differently?

To answer this question, let's consider another unactualised possibility. Let's imagine that you almost landed the perfect job. You learn later that, as far as the search committee was concerned, you and the successful candidate were both equally qualified. In the end, they had to flip a coin in order to make a decision. The job was practically yours, it can seem, but then you were robbed by blind fate. Similarly, when you contemplate your mother having an abortion, you are imagining a situation in which all of the events over the aeons had managed to lead up to the union of one particular egg and one particular sperm, a union which, if your mother had not had an abortion, would have developed into you. It can seem, then, that, when you imagine your mother having an abortion, you are imagining her, not blindly, but knowingly, taking away from you a significant good – life itself – that was already and rightfully yours.

But was it really? The job wasn't really yours, though it's easy to imagine it being yours. You existed; the job existed. Had events gone just slightly differently, the job would have been yours; but they didn't go differently, the job wasn't yours, and so it was never taken away from you. In order for a life (or part of a life) to be taken away from you, there has to be a *you* from which it is taken. When circumstances didn't conspire to bring into existence the merely possible people that I asked you to imagine, they weren't harmed, because in order to be an object of harm, one has to be an object. And in order to be an object, one has to exist. They never did. So when you imagine your mother having had an abortion, are you imagining suffering the terrible harm of your life being taken away from you, *or* are you instead imagining the possibility of your never having existed at all and so never having been a candidate for harm?

The answer to this question depends, of course, on when *you* came into existence, and the answer to this question depends on what features make you *you*. Did you exist once that particular egg and that particular sperm got together? Did you come into existence when that fertilised ovum developed into a foetus with some mental properties? Did you come into existence only when that foetus developed into a being with more sophisticated mental capabilities? These are very difficult and complex philosophical questions which I cannot explore here. My own (undefended) views are these. Although we tend to think of our existence as an all-or-nothing kind of thing, I believe that the boundaries that mark our beginning and end are not at all sharp. Nonetheless, I also believe that, however vague these boundaries, there was clearly a *you* before you acquired sophisticated mental capabilities. Once you exist, the ending of your life constitutes a harm that is done to you. And, I agree, the earlier your life is ended, the more significant your loss.

Part III

What May I Hope?

'Every art and every inquiry, and similarly every action and pursuit, is thought to aim at some good; and for this reason the good has rightly been declared to be that at which all things aim . . . If, then, there is some end of the things we do, which we desire for its own sake (everything else being desired for the sake of this), and if we do not choose everything for the sake of something else (for at that rate the process would go on to infinity, so that our desire would be empty and vain), clearly this must be the good and the chief good. Will not the knowledge of it, then, have a great influence on life? Shall we not, like archers who have a mark to aim at, be more likely to hit upon what is right? If so, we must try, in outline at least, to determine what it is, and of which of the sciences or capacities it is the object.'

– Aristotle, *Nicomachean Ethics*

'The reflective person feels a grief that the unreflective do not know, a grief that can well lead to moral ruination: this is a discontentedness with the providence that governs the entire course of the world; and he feels it when he thinks about the evil that so greatly oppresses the human race, leaving it without (apparent) hope for something better. It is of the greatest importance, however, to be content with providence (even though it has marked out for us so toilsome a road through this earthly world), partly so that we can always take courage under our burdens and – since we push guilt for those burdens off on fate and not ourselves, who may perhaps be the sole cause of these evils – fix our eyes on that fact and not neglect our own obligation to contribute to the betterment of ourselves.'

– Immanuel Kant, 'Speculative Beginning of Human History'

Q

66 *I am contemplating having children, yet can think of no good reason to have them. It seems impossible to have obligations toward a person who doesn't exist yet, so are there any good reasons to have children that aren't selfish?* 99

A

Nicholas D. Smith: I think some philosophers would argue that there are good reasons not to have children, given population pressures. But I am inclined to take a rather different tack here, by asking you why you seem to suppose that self-interest is the same as the vice of selfishness. One of the things I found extraordinary in my own experience of having children was how much love I found I was capable of having and sharing. Did that bring value to my own life? Most certainly it did! Did it bring value to the lives of others? I think (and hope) so. Did I become a better person, all things considered? I think (and hope) so. And if I am doing a good job with my children (as I hope I am), then everyone with whom they come into contact is potentially better off. Plainly, not all parents are good people, and parenting does not always improve those who do it. But if you desire to have children, I think that is at least one indication that you could do something that is valuable not just for yourself but for many others, including not just the children you bring into being. Don't underestimate the power of love, especially if the one who has it is also ethically conscientious!

Q

" According to Goethe, the only people who are truly happy are those who are like children. What would fulfil the requirements of being like children, and how would that make you happy? "

A

Nalini Bhushan: The image of the happy child is often invoked as a model for adult happiness (you mention Goethe; Nietzsche, in *Thus Spake Zarathustra*, in the section on the three metamorphoses, for instance, does so as well). While this may in the end constitute an overly romantic view of a child's world, the model as such has going for it at least the following intriguing components:

1. *Spontaneity of action*: Children, it is said, lack a complex inner life, so that their responses to events are immediate, near-instinctive, and without the quality of angst that can often accompany adult retrospective analyses of actions taken.
2. *Orientation to the here-now*: Connected to the first component, children lack the baggage of the past, and, importantly, have less ability to concretely imagine their futures (although they no doubt have rich imaginations),

so that their perspective tends for the most part to be oriented towards the present rather than the past or the future.

3. *Ease of verbal and bodily expression*: Lacking consciousness of the gaze of others, children freely navigate the physical, auditory, olfactory and verbal spaces they inhabit.

Does this model of the happy child give adults ideas as to how to make ourselves happy? Perhaps.

First, there is a kind of freedom that an adult could well experience in virtue of being able to act in a situation by assessing it swiftly and with clarity at the outset, without the conscious intervention of a range of beliefs and desires that typically precede (and at times stultify) adult action. Second, the model prescribes a heavier weighting of the present than of either the past or the future as a component of happiness. It forces us to ask what it is that one does see, as an adult, as one scrutinises one's own current (and past) life and contemplates one's future, and to ask whether all of that is really relevant to one's current life. It may help to pry us away from the felt heaviness of past decisions and commitments, and to ask: am I really stuck with a certain way of doing things or are there options currently before me that I cannot *see*? And, third, it may get us to reduce the inhibitions we place on what we express with our voices and our bodies, and in this way to reduce stress. (There are currently laugh clubs all over India, where the goal is to engage in belly-heaving laughter for no good reason, and karaoke bars all over East Asia, where businessmen can sing their hearts out at the end of a gruelling day.)

Q

❝ *Why are some emotions looked down upon? Why isn't it just as good to be happy as to be sad?* **❞**

A

Nalini Bhushan: A central reason is that certain parts of our culture associate sadness or sorrow with the possession of a depth of character, and happiness with a certain superficiality. For instance, a person who is alive to sorrow is taken to be capable of discerning the true nature of things, of seeing people for who they really are, of seeing the world for the random and chaotic place that it really is, appearances of planning or design notwithstanding. In this way, sorrow becomes the emotional marker of depth of character. In contrast, a happy person is often viewed as seeing at best what lies on the surface, or on what is most easily accessible to him or her. This character trait is in turn often associated with an attraction to the material, whether it be with how things look (beautiful cars, bodies, houses) or with what one can acquire with money, rather than with the things that attract one's heart, mind or soul.

There is, however, another weighting one can give to happiness and sorrow, one that we find in other cultures or traditions. In the Buddhist tradition, for instance, sorrow or suffering is indeed a fundamental aspect of the human condition, so that the person who experiences sorrow is more enlightened than the person who merrily goes through life without ever experiencing this emotion. But it is the mark of a person of greater enlightenment to be able, upon experiencing those aspects of the human condition that cause one sorrow (like sickness, death, loss of various kinds) to accept and then rise above these to a state of happiness, tranquillity, and even joy.

On this view, in the end, happiness would be valued more than sorrow, for it is based upon a fuller, complete and more complex understanding of experience. And the joyful person would be better able to experience than the person whose heart is full of sorrow what is a central emotion for the Buddhist, namely compassion, which requires an openness and receptivity to the plight and emotional states of others.

Q

Is it possible to measure sorrow or happiness? If so, can one person's grief or joy be greater than another's?

A

Mark Crimmins: This is one of those questions where your first impulse is to say 'Of course!' and 'Impossible!' at the same time (which is of course impossible). Of course! We have little trouble discerning that the suicidal depressive is less cheery than the tiny tot with her eyes all aglow. We're very confident even about much subtler discriminations: for instance, that runner who has finally achieved his personal best is more elated than this chef who is satisfied that her new dish will maintain the restaurant's reputation. But, impossible! We can never get the chef's satisfaction into the same mind as the runner's excitement. And don't we have to be able to do that to compare them? Couldn't it be that the chef's joy is far greater, and yet she reacts to that level of joy in a far more subdued way than the runner would (perhaps her 'baseline' mood would make the runner skip and sing)?

Maybe brain science can help us? Suppose we've determined experimentally (imagine a really enormous and exceptionally well-designed study) that there is an extremely tight match between the level of a certain chemical C in the

brain and the degree to which careful observers of sponta-
neously-acting people take them to be feeling joy. Suppose it
is further discovered that C-levels are responsible for the
paradigmatic physiological effects of joy, and even its paradigmatic cognitive effects (perhaps these include optimistic
thinking, high energy levels, generosity, and so on). Then,
couldn't we conclude, with some confidence, that C-levels
provide a measure of joy itself? I think some philosophers
would answer, 'Absolutely!' Of these, some would reason that
joy is whatever it is that actually plays a certain causal role:
that of producing joyful behaviour and joyful cognitive
dispositions; and we would have discovered that high C-
levels do this; so joy *is* having a high C-level. Others would
reason (only subtly differently) that joy is having *some or
other* state that plays that causal role, so we would have
discovered that having a high C-level is *how joy happens in
humans*. Both camps would conclude that joy is measurable
and comparable between people. Another camp of philosophers would dissent. They would insist that what's been
correlated with C-levels isn't joy itself, but its behavioural
and cognitive effects. Who's to say that the very same 'joyful'
behaviour and cognitive dispositions might not be produced
by vastly different amounts of joy in different people? Still
other philosophers would shake their heads at the naïvety of
the rest of us for treating an ordinary word like 'joy' as if
there's any hope for the idea that there's some 'aspect of
reality' that it labels.

Stay tuned for the answer. We'll have it for you in a century
or two, easily.

Q

66 According to statistics, one in five people experiences depression. If depression is so common, how do we know that it is an illness and not just a normal part of being human? Perhaps it's not reasonable to expect to be happy! 99

A

Marc Lange: That is an excellent question. The distinction between health and illness is tremendously controversial. Some philosophers believe that the difference is established entirely by various facts about the natural world. These philosophers might point out that insofar as depression arises from the production of certain extreme quantities of some neurotransmitter or from some particular gene, which ultimately inhibits or prevents certain cells from carrying out their basic life functions (e.g., from employing a certain metabolic pathway to derive energy), then depression has a biochemical basis. On this view, that depression is common does not change the fact that it involves the malfunctioning of some part of the body, where 'malfunctioning' can be understood in terms drawn entirely from biology.

(But what, then, *does* it mean for a part of the body to function properly? What determines the body part's biological function? That, too, is a controversial question. One suggestion is that a body part's functioning properly involve its doing what it has been naturally selected to do over the course of recent evolutionary history. The heart's function is to pump the blood, not to make 'lub dub' sounds (though it does that, too), because its pumping the blood is what has contributed to the survival and reproductive success of creatures with hearts.)

Other philosophers disagree. They believe that the distinction between health and illness rests on certain value-judgments, not entirely on biological facts. These value-judgments are reflected in which conditions society considers it appropriate to consult a doctor about, or in which conditions people regard as undesirable. Again, that depression is common does not in any way conflict with its being regarded as undesirable.

Of course, one might believe that value-judgments inevitably play a role in distinguishing health from disease, and yet also hold that the distinction between health and disease is not merely 'in the eye of the beholder' because certain value-judgments are objectively correct and others are objectively mistaken. For instance, runaway slaves were diagnosed in antebellum South Carolina as having a disease ('drapetomania') that caused them to run away. We now consider this classification of runaway slaves to be wildly inaccurate, and our value-judgments have everything to do with why. That slavery is morally wrong and that a slave's intense desire to escape her predicament is perfectly understandable may be among our value-judgments. But they are not *mere* value-judgments. We believe strongly that these judgments are objectively correct, not merely a matter of our taste.

In whatever way health and illness are characterised, the fact that one in five people experiences depression does not conflict with the idea that depression is an illness. After all, a great many people have cavities in their teeth, but cavities still constitute illnesses, not instances of good health. Remember that 'depression' in the medical sense is distinct from feeling the blues. If there is 'a good reason' for someone to feel down, then it is probably not depression in the medical sense.

Q

66 *Should we lose our faith in God because of events like Hurricane Katrina?* **99**

A

Louise Antony: Your question is a version of a philosophical challenge to theism known as 'The Problem of Evil': how could an all-powerful, perfectly good Being permit suffering to occur? If God is unable to prevent it, then God must not be all-powerful; if God can prevent it, but chooses not to, then God must not be perfectly good.

This objection really has two forms. One form is strictly logical: it challenges the believer to show how the existence of an all-powerful, all-knowing, and perfectly benevolent being is not inconsistent with the existence of suffering in our world. The challenge in this form can be met rather easily. All that must be done is to deny that suffering is a bad thing. This can be done in a number of ways: one can argue, for example, that we only regard suffering as bad because we fail to understand God's larger purpose in allowing suffering – perhaps, it's actually good, because it leads to greater wisdom than we'd obtain otherwise. Or, it can be argued that 'suffering' is only a relative notion, and that if there is any variation at all in the amount of pleasure we experience, we will always regard the least amount as 'suffering'. I don't think either of these responses is very effective, but they suffice to show that there's nothing incoherent about believing in God while acknowledging the existence of (what we commonly regard as) suffering.

The second form of the problem of evil is very different. In this version, the challenge is to the reasonableness, rather than to the mere coherence of, belief in an all-powerful, all-knowing, perfectly benevolent being, given the existence of suffering. The question here is this: if we were to examine the evidence objectively and dispassionately, would we come to the conclusion that the universe was created by such a perfectly good, omnipotent Being, or would we come to some different conclusion? A conclusion such as: the universe was created by a perfectly benevolent being who had limited knowledge or limited power, or both? Or that it was created by a being who was completely indifferent to our feelings? Or that it wasn't created according to any intentional plan at all, but just 'happened'? Thought of this way, the problem of evil is a challenge to the believer to show that evidence and reason supports belief in the Judeo-Christian God, and supports it above its competitor hypotheses.

It's worth noting in this connection that the argument for the existence of God that has the most popular support – the argument for 'intelligent design' – can only show that the Creator is smart enough and powerful enough to have made a universe. It doesn't even purport to show that the Creator is morally good.

My own view is that there is no evidence whatsoever that the designer of our universe (if there was one) was concerned in the slightest about the welfare of the sentient creatures He/

She/It was creating, and that there's mountains of evidence that He/She/It couldn't give a damn.

One final observation: believers often like to have it both ways. One person will thank God for sparing him, while telling the neighbour whose home's been demolished that it's not God's fault. But this doesn't make sense. If God actually intervened to save the first person's home, then shame on Him for not doing the same for the second person's. And if the reason that He didn't save the second person's is that the poor bugger's homelessness was part of some unfathomable Divine Plan, then the first person shouldn't take things personally either. The only way out of this dilemma that I can see is to say that each person deserved what they got – i.e., bad things don't happen to good people. If anyone says this, they have, in my view, left the company of decent people.

Q

66 *Could God make a rock so heavy that He couldn't lift it? If He could, then He isn't all powerful. But if He can't make such a rock, then it also seems He's not all powerful. Either way, there's something God cannot do. So, it seems that God (or anything for that matter) can't be omnipotent.* **99**

A

Richard Heck: This is a version of an old problem, one discussed endlessly by theologians. In its simplest form, it goes like this: can God make a rock that is both big and not big? Obviously not. So God isn't omnipotent.

The most popular response to this question, which was favoured by Thomas Aquinas, is that we have to be more careful about how we understand omnipotence. To be omnipotent isn't to be able to do absolutely anything: it's to be able to do anything *that can possibly be done.* Could God make a rock that was both big and not big? No, but God's inability to do so is no threat to God's omnipotence, since there simply couldn't be a rock that was both big and not big. Likewise, if God is omnipotent, then it simply isn't possible for there to be a rock so big that He can't lift it. So it's no limit on God's power if He can't create a rock so big that He can't lift it.

It is worth mentioning, as well, that some philosophers – René Descartes, for example – have held that God *could* make a rock that is both big and not big! On this view, God's powers are completely unlimited, so much so that God is not bound even by the laws of logic. It may be impossible for us to understand how that is so, but that is because our minds are finite, whereas the Creator's is infinite.

Q

66 *Is faith in something intangible ultimately delusional?* **99**

A

Alexander George: Is this another way of asking whether belief in the existence of God must be irrational in the light of God's intangibility? If so, I would answer No. There are many things that I cannot touch in whose existence it's reasonable for me to believe. For instance, I believe in the existence of Mars, but I'll never touch it.

You might think that's a bad example because, while I can't actually touch Mars, I could in principle touch it: in theory, I could build a spaceship that will bring me to Mars. God, on the other hand, seems to be something that I couldn't even in principle touch: according to many, God simply isn't located anywhere in the physical universe.

But *don't* we believe in the existence of intangible things even in that stronger sense of 'intangible'? For instance, most of us believe that the Equator exists, but it's not tangible: for instance, I can't trip over the Equator. Most of us think that numbers, like the number 8, exist, even though they aren't located in the physical realm: they cannot be touched or seen, for instance. So if one is irrational to believe in God's existence, that's not because God is something intangible.

But perhaps you meant to be asking whether it's irrational to believe in an intangible God's existence *on the basis of no evidence*. If a person thinks the answer to that question is Yes, then God's intangibility again seems irrelevant: that person would likewise hold that it's not rational to believe in a *tangible* object's existence if one had no evidence at all for it. If there is something non-rational here, its source is our lack of evidence and not the intangibility of the being that is believed to exist.

Q

Given that there is no proof either way, is it any more valid to say 'There is a God' than it is to say 'There is no God'? Or is the only valid claim 'I don't know if there is a God'?

A

Louise Antony: There's a common misconception about 'proof' – that if a statement cannot be 'proven', then it's equally rational to believe either it or its negation. If 'prove' means 'establish with logical certainty from self-evident first principles', then nothing outside mathematics, logic and semantics can be proven. (It's even a matter of controversy whether anything *within* mathematics, logic and semantics can be proven.) So the class of statements that cannot be *proven* is very, very big, and includes all of the following: 'There is no Santa Claus,' 'Dogs are animals,' 'Washington, DC is the capital of the United States,' and 'Salt is soluble in water.' But surely you believe all of these things, and would find foolish anyone who withheld judgment about them just because they could not be *proven*.

So the real issue, for any proposition, is what the arguments are. There are certainly many arguments for the existence of God, and many against, most of which are quite accessible to any thoughtful person (unlike the considerations for and against, say, string theory in physics, which can only be evaluated by experts). Given this, it would only be reasonable to conclude that one cannot know if God exists if the arguments all turned out to be very weak (so that you have no reason to go either way) or if they turned out to be equally strong (so that you have reasons to go in two contradictory directions). I happen to think that there are no *good* arguments *for* belief in God and one extremely compelling argument *against* it – the argument from evil.

I get the feeling from some people I know who call themselves 'agnostics' that they think they are being more modest, or less dogmatic, than either theists or atheists. Maybe they think they're hedging their bets in regard to the afterlife. In any case, I'm the kind of atheist who thinks that God most respects the people who apportion their beliefs to the evidence.

Q

" *If God's will is ultimately unknowable, then how can we know what is morally right?* "

A

David Brink: Dostoevsky's character Ivan Karamazov reputedly believes that if God is dead then everything is permitted. Of course, permission is itself one kind of moral status. So, taken literally, this dictum claims that atheism entails a very permissive and, hence, very revisionary moral code. A more common view is that there could be no objective moral code whatsoever without God's will. This assumes that there could be no objective moral requirements without divine command. This assumption would explain the frequent appeal to religious scholars and members of the clergy as authorities on issues of moral significance. It would also explain why, despite the liberal democratic tradition of the separation of church and state, many people, including members of the United States judiciary, sometimes assert that constitutional rights depend upon divine command. These people assume that morality requires a religious foundation and deny the *autonomy* of ethics.

But there are good reasons to deny the assumption that morality requires a religious foundation and to assert the autonomy of ethics. It is not just that atheism and agnosticism do not preclude recognition of moral requirements. Even theists have reason for thinking that morality is independent of religion. Socrates long ago asked whether something was right because God commanded it or whether God commanded it because it was right (the famous question asked in Plato's dialogue *Euthyphro*). Socrates reasoned that God's will could not make something valuable, because that would leave both value and God's preferences contingent and arbitrary. Instead, Socrates concluded, the theist should say that God commands what he does, because he himself is good. On this view, God's commands are principled and track what is independently valuable. This also explains why theists often feel compelled to resolve debates about what God has willed, and how we can ascertain his will, by appeal to our moral ideas about what a morally good God could have willed. For, in doing so, they explain God's will by appeal to morality, not morality by appeal to God's will. If so, one can see how religion might presuppose morality; it's harder to see how morality presupposes religion.

This is to recognise the autonomy of ethics. But the autonomy of ethics implies that there should be no deep puzzle about how there could be an objective morality without God, because plausible versions of theism must themselves recognise an objective morality – that is, one independent of God's will.

The autonomy of ethics, however, means that moral requirements do not depend on God's will. So we do not need to settle moral perplexity by trying to ascertain God's will. How, then, should we reason morally? Here, as elsewhere, it makes sense to begin, at least provisionally, with what we are most confident about. We could start with widely shared rules about nonmaleficence, beneficence, honesty, fidelity and fair play. We could then try to revise and extend these rules in principled ways. The idea would be to treat these common moral rules much as judges, lawyers and other interpreters treat common-law decisions. We look for principles that explain patterns in our existing decisions and rules. It may be that not all existing materials fit into a coherent pattern. If so, the principles that subsume and explain the most decisions and rules may require us to view some of them as mistaken. Moreover, part of accepting a principle is adhering to it in novel situations. So we test rival principles not only by how well they accommodate existing rules and decisions but also by how plausibly they project to new and perplexing cases. In this common-law fashion, we might use analogical reasoning from common moral rules to interpret, revise and extend the guidance that these rules provide. For instance, it was presumably something like this sort of analogical reasoning from the parochial outward that has led to the progressive extension of equal concern and respect to women, other races, other religions, etc.

Whether or not God is dead (does not exist), the autonomy of ethics implies that we can and should do our best to identify and conform to moral principles that provide this sort of reflectively acceptable guidance.

Q

❝ *A lot of people say that they believe in God because otherwise there would have been nothing that made the universe: 'It had to come from somewhere!' they say. But if that's what you're basing your beliefs on, then shouldn't you want to know who made God? And who made the being who made God?* **❞**

A

Alexander George: You've made an important observation: explaining why X exists by postulating the existence of Y doesn't take one far if the very questions one had about X's existence can be raised about Y's.

Philosophers like to tell the story of the sage who was asked why the Earth didn't fall through the heavens. He said: 'Because it sits on the back of a giant turtle.' His questioner was still a little puzzled and asked the sage what kept the giant turtle from falling through the heavens. The sage answered: 'It sits on the back of another giant turtle.' His questioner remained puzzled and so asked what kept this second giant turtle from falling through the heavens. 'Ah,' the sage said, 'it's turtles all the way down!' Obviously, turtles all the way down doesn't seem satisfactory.

Of course, the sage might instead have replied: 'The first giant turtle has no need of support!' But if that turtle has no need for support, then why not just say that the Earth doesn't either?

A

Sean Greenberg: A version of the story about the sage is deployed by John Locke in Book II of his great *Essay Concerning Human Understanding*, in order to show why the concept of substance makes no sense. Locke's aim, in recounting the story, is to attack the idea that there is a distinction between substance and its attributes or properties. His point is that once you remove the properties of a thing, that thing no longer exists. One can see what his point is by undertaking the following exercise of imagination. (The technical philosophical term for such an exercise of imagination is 'thought experiment'.) Imagine a red ball. Now imagine that red ball, neither red, nor round. What are you imagining? Nothing. Locke claims that the notion of substance, as distinct from properties, has no more content than the imagination of a red ball that is neither red nor round. He says that such a notion is the notion of 'something, I know not what'.

Most theists would not take such considerations to apply to God, because God is a *causa sui*, a cause of his own existence. In this respect, God differs from all finite beings.

The following question arises, however: why should we believe that God is the one and only *causa sui*? Well, imagine that some other being were the cause of God's existence. Then that other being would be more powerful than God. But that can't be: God is the most powerful of all beings. Hence, no other being could be the cause of God's existence. If God exists, then He must be the cause of His own existence.

Q

‹‹ *Is it possible to deify any object, perhaps a penguin? If so, what qualities or properties would make the object a fit candidate for deification?* **››**

A

Sean Greenberg: In Chapter XII of his masterpiece *Leviathan*, Hobbes says that 'there is almost nothing that has a name that has not been esteemed . . . in one place or another, a god or a devil . . . Men, women, a bird, a crocodile, a calf, a dog, a snake, an onion, a leek [were] deified.' Although the first documented penguin sightings occurred on Vasco da Gama's 1497 expedition along the southern coast of Africa, Hobbes himself doesn't mention penguins in *Leviathan*. However, there is no reason why penguins would be any less fit candidates for deification than birds, calves, onions or leeks. It is certainly possible to deify a penguin; given that there is a word 'penguin', Hobbes would probably say that penguins have been deified somewhere by now.

According to Hobbes, the deification of men, women, birds, crocodiles, calves, etc. is due to human ignorance of the nature of God. Consequently, Hobbes – and most Christians – would say that one would not be justified in deifying any of these beings, including penguins, because only a being with all the attributes of the Christian God (omniscience, omnipotence, etc.) is justly worshipped, but no finite being has such attributes, and consequently, no finite being ought to be worshipped. Indeed, no monotheistic religion would allow penguins to be deified. Only in a polytheistic religion would it be appropriate to deify, and worship, a penguin. (I don't, however, know of any religions in which penguins figure.)

Q

66 *Why do humans always put a higher value on material goods (like diamonds and gold) than life?* **99**

A

Nicholas D. Smith: Valuing material goods even more than life itself, I think most (if not all) philosophers would agree, is a very serious and ultimately self-defeating ethical error. It is, very simply, to assign greater value to what is in fact far less valuable. But there may also be another error here. If we think that life has *intrinsic* value (as many, but not all, philosophers do), then valuing wealth over life itself is to mistake something that has *only* instrumental value – value, that is, only for the pursuit or acquisition of something *else* that is valuable – for something that is *intrinsically valuable* (valuable, that is, just in and of itself and not only for trying to obtain something else).

It is generally agreed that wealth is *only* instrumentally valuable. Just think: if someone were to give you a million dollars, but only under the stipulation that you (and your heirs, and their heirs, etc.) could *never* spend it on anything, what real *value* would the money have (for you or for anyone else)? The value of money *just is* whatever it enables you to do or to purchase – it *just is* the instrumental value it provides for getting other things. You might think, however, that just being alive is valuable (consider the alternative!).

Of course, there may be other intrinsic values that could come into conflict with the value of life itself. We value not being in pain or suffering, for example, such that unrelieved suffering might lead us to conclude that life itself is no longer valuable enough to continue. But such cases do not show that life is not intrinsically valuable, only that there can be considerations that can trump its value.

Some philosophers, however, have said that life is not intrinsically valuable, but can only become valuable if it is lived in certain ways. So Socrates famously said that 'the unexamined life is not worth living for a human being' (in Plato's *Apology*), which seems to suggest that he did not think that life itself was intrinsically valuable, but gained value only by being or becoming an 'examined' life (one in which critical inquiry was a significant feature is what he meant, I think).

Anyway, it is generally foolish and self-defeating to live one's life as if something that is simply of instrumental value were actually intrinsically valuable, or brought value to a life just by its acquisition. Imagine thinking that one's life would be clearly enriched by acquiring every tool known to humankind, by one who had no clue as to how to *use* those tools! If one could figure out what was really valuable (intrinsically valuable, that is), maybe then one could figure out how to use money in such a way as to put the money to good use!

Q

66 *If no one ever loves me during my lifetime – if I don't ever have a relationship – will I have not lived a good life? Is love that important to life, or is it something you can choose to engage in if you like?* **99**

A

Jyl Gentzler: The answer to this question depends on what makes a life good. Of course, many philosophers have offered helpful suggestions, but all of these suggestions, as far as I can tell, are simply variations on theories articulated long ago by the Ancient Greeks.

One currently popular conception of the good life, hedonism, is defended by the character Socrates in Plato's dialogue *Protagoras*. One counts as having lived a good life if over a lifetime one has experienced a sufficient quantity of pleasure that is not counter-balanced by experiences of pain. On this view, relationships aren't valuable in themselves. Whether they contribute to the goodness of your life will depend on whether you are the sort of person to take pleasure in relationships or are constantly overwhelmed by anxiety and fear of rejection. It will also depend on your luck and skill with relationships: some people are just more pleasant than others, and it is typically very painful when good relationships (and even not so good relationships) end. And, finally, whether relationships contribute to the goodness of your life will depend on what other options are available to you that might bring you more pleasure and less pain over the course of your lifetime.

I myself am not convinced by hedonism. Let's imagine that I believe about myself that I am widely admired and deeply loved by my friends and family and that this belief gives me deep feelings of contentment and satisfaction. But let's imagine also that I am completely deluded: I am ridiculed behind my back and privately despised by my friends and family who are hoping to receive a big inheritance from me. Let's suppose further that their secret is safe. I would think that no matter how much pleasure I experience in my delusion, I am not living a good life. Perhaps this judgment is due to the fact that I care about much more than the subjective quality – viz., whether they are painful or pleasurable – of my own subjective mental states. I care, for example, about the welfare of my children, my own grip on reality, and my own standing in the community. If my children don't do well, if I'm seriously deluded, and if I'm privately despised, then (whether I'm aware of these facts or not, and so whether I feel mental distress about my situation or not) I myself am not living a life that is good for me.

These sorts of considerations have led some philosophers to conclude that a good life is not a matter of a positive balance of pleasure over pain, but instead is a matter of desire-satisfaction. Even if I'm not aware of the fact that my desires have not been satisfied, to the extent that they are not satisfied, I am worse off, and to the extent that they are satisfied, I am better off. (Plato explores this conception of a good life in his *Gorgias*.) On this conception of a good life, whether relationships are important to your life will depend on whether you have any desire for a relationship and also on whether any given relationship will help you to satisfy other desires that you have or, instead, will frustrate them. Perhaps you have no burning desire to have a relationship with Mary, but Mary is well-connected, and if you fool her into thinking that you care for her, she will do what is required to satisfy your deep desires for status and power. In these circumstances, on the desire-satisfaction account of a good life, having a good life may well demand that you deceive and exploit Mary in this way.

However, others have thought that I could fail to live a good life even if I were experiencing a lot of pleasure and even if the desires that I had were satisfied. The most famous view of this sort is the one that Aristotle endorsed in his *Nicomachean Ethics*. If I were to reduce my desires to those of a grazing animal (e.g., a cow), Aristotle observes, then it may well be the case that all of the desires that I possess would be satisfied and that I would experience a great deal of pleasure and no pain. Nonetheless, he predicted, no one would consider me fortunate. I would be regarded not with envy, but instead with pity. To be considered well-off, Aristotle believed, I (a human being) must live a life that is suitable for a human being. According to Aristotle, a life that did not involve friendships would not be a life that is suitable for a human being. Further, on Aristotle's view, relationships such as the one that I imagined you having with Mary do not in themselves contribute to a good life. Genuine friends care about the goodness of their friends' lives, for their friends' own sake, and you (I am imagining) are treating Mary not as a friend but as a tool. For a human to treat another human being in this way is ugly, and so detracts from the best sort of life for a human.

I think that there is much to be said for such a view. On Aristotle's view, in order to determine whether Bob is living a good life, we first need to determine what kind of creature Bob is, e.g., is he a human being, a dog or an oak tree? We then would judge the quality of his life against a species standard of flourishing. For example, our view of what it would mean for a dog to live a good life is informed by our views about the nature of dogs. We tend to think of a dog who lives its life in a cage as not living a good life for a dog, even if we imagine that it is given sufficient drugs to feel no discontent or frustration. A good life for a dog, we think, would be one that involved companionship, running around, barking at threatening noises and strangers, and so forth. Because a dog in a cage on drugs is not given the opportunity to engage in doggy activities, it is not functioning as a dog at a high level, and so is not living a good life for a dog. If Bob is a dog, Aristotle would say, then we would consider his life as good for him just in case he both had a lot of opportunities to engage in doggy activities and performed doggily at a high level. If Bob were a human being, however, we would not judge his life as going well if he spent his life running around with other dogs and barking at threatening noises and strangers, no matter how well he performed at these activities. There's something wrong with Bob, we'd think; and even if he is content with his doggy life, since he's a human being, he's not living a good life.

However, we might wonder whether Aristotle is right to judge the quality of an individual person's life against a species standard. Ultimately, I think, whether something counts as good *for me* depends only on facts *about me*, and not on facts about the other organisms who happened to be grouped with me for the purposes of biological explanations. While I agree with Aristotle that, in order to know what would be a good life for me, I would first need to figure out what sort of creature I am, and while I agree that it is likely that as a human being my nature will be very similar to the nature of other human beings, I don't agree that the quality of my life should be judged in terms of its conformity to what would be a good life for most normal human beings. I might be quite unusual in that I am, by nature, unable to feel affection for, or enjoy the company of, other human beings. To be sure, if I were of this abnormal sort, life in a human society would be difficult, since others would have expectations of me that would be mistaken. And it is no doubt generally true that, for human beings, it would be easier to live a good life if one were normal in this respect. However, it doesn't follow from this fact about the practical difficulties of such abnormality that my life would go better for me if it involved loving relationships. If my nature were idiosyncratic in the way that I described, then loving relationships just would be no part of what would constitute a good life for me and I could live a perfectly good life without them.

Q

❝ Does the value of a person's life decrease as his age increases? Wouldn't most people choose to save a two-year-old over a 60-year-old? Is there any justification for this? ❞

A

Nicholas D. Smith: As the old joke goes . . . Hey! I resemble that!

As someone pushing 60 myself, I guess my first reaction is to say that I most certainly *do not* think my life now has less value than that of a two-year-old. Nor do I think the value of a human life is measurable in terms of how many (more) years the person will live.

Answers to this sort of question will differ on the basis of which style of moral theory one applies to it. In a *consequentialist* view, a human life will be valuable in terms of the overall balance of benefits and harms that derive from it: people who do really good things will have really valuable lives, and those who don't, won't . . . and people who do really bad things will have lives that have negative value. A 20-year-old criminal, in this view, would have a life that was worth much less than Mother Teresa's life, even when she was getting very old. In other accounts, all human lives are equal in value. So, according to Kant's categorical imperative, we should treat *all* people as if they were ends only, and not means to ends. One's age would not seem to be a factor in this way of estimating things. In virtue theory, the value of one's life would depend upon the qualities of one's character. So again, in this view, a good person (of any age) would have a more valuable life than a bad one (of any age).

At any rate, I am inclined to think that the relative values of human lives (if there really are different values to different human lives) will not be determined solely by age. But maybe I just say that because . . . well . . . I am getting on in years!

Q

66 *If every life ends in death, then how could life have any value?* **99**

A

Peter Lipton: The value of life comes from what you do in your life: your activities and achievements. These are real even though you die, and would be no more real if you lived for ever (though admittedly you would have time for a lot more of them).

A

Alexander George: Kant spoke of those who 'fear death without loving life, and who, despite their difficulty in bringing the most middling contentment to each day of their existence, nonetheless never have enough days to go through the torment again'. The same holds for value. If your life now has no point to it, then having a lot more of such a life isn't going to improve the situation. A whole lot of nothing doesn't amount to much.

A

Peter S. Fosl: This is a compelling question. Recently, a student of mine broached a similar question during a discussion we were having about the condition the universe seems to be heading towards. It seems, I'm told, that everything in the universe will ultimately degenerate into a vast, endless, more-or-less uniform, horribly cold and dark field of low-level radiation. Some call this condition, the final destination of the universe, 'entropic hell'.

In the light of this apparent fact, the relevant question concerning the value of life is this: since everything we accomplish will ultimately be destroyed and degenerate into 'entropic hell', what value can anything have?

I think there's something misleading about his question, however, something that lurks in a hidden assumption that the question makes. The question and its force rely largely on the assumption that life has value only if it lasts for ever. In my view, this is a dubious assumption, and indeed one that plagues a good deal of our culture's thinking about value.

Far from being a necessary condition for value, I think that immortality and endless existence would actually undermine the value of life.

Consider the issue this way: would life be as valuable or even valuable at all if it weren't finite? That is, if we lived for ever, would much or anything matter to us? Perhaps the avoidance of physical pain would still matter, but simply not being in pain seems to be a relatively meaningless affair. Don't many of our projects have value for us just because we know that one day we and they will come to an end?

The very fragility of things gives us reason to care what happens to them, to defend them and us against harm or diminishment. When you can just start over or always have a substitute, things don't really matter. Because things are finite, and we know we're going to die, our actions count. We'd better get things right because we're not going to get another shot.

Q

66 *What is the meaning of life? If one believes in evolution, is there no answer to this question? Must one believe in 'Intelligent Design' to be able to answer it?* **99**

A

Richard Heck: 'What is the meaning of life?' The question is almost a joke, isn't it? But there's probably no question that is more strongly identified with philosophy than that one. I wouldn't for a moment pretend to be able to answer it. Fortunately, however, the question here isn't what the meaning of life is but simply whether life can have a meaning in the absence of some intelligence behind the creation of life, the universe and everything.

But before we can address that question, we need to address the question of what 'the meaning of life' is supposed to mean. It's an odd phrase. Words have meaning; art has meaning – but life? What on earth does one want to know when one asks what the meaning of life is? I take it that the question is supposed to be what the purpose or point of life is. If so, however, that's an odd way to ask the question. Why think that life, as such, has any uniform point or purpose? Does the life of a plant have the same point as that of an animal? That of a penguin the same as that of a gnu? What difference would it make one way or the other? Or is it just human life whose point or purpose is in question? And if so, why?

I suspect that people who have asked what 'the meaning of life' is have wanted some understanding of what they were supposed to be doing with their lives. The cover of Killing Joke's second album shows a young lad looking up at the sky and screaming the album's title: 'What's This For . . . !?' That's the feeling behind the question. If we knew what the meaning of life was, the thought might be, then we'd have some idea of what the goal of life was, and that would give us some sense of what a well-lived life would be like. Then we'd have some idea what we ought to be doing.

So there's a question: what ought one to do with one's life? Or, simpler still: how ought one to live?

Does life have to have a point, or a purpose, or a meaning for this question to have an answer? I don't see why. It's not at all obvious that there has to be some goal everyone is supposed to be trying to reach for there to be some sensible answer to the question how one ought to live. If not, however, then I don't see why there being a sensible answer to the question depends upon life's having been created by some intelligence rather than having evolved. That isn't, of course, to say that how one thinks one ought to live won't depend in any way upon whether one believes in God or in what kind of God one believes.

Indeed, in the end, the real question here seems to be an intensely personal one. How ought I to live? What ought I to do with my life? We all have to struggle with such questions, and I would pity anyone who did not. But, if that is what the question about the meaning of life asks in the end, then I'm not sure it really is a question that should be strongly identified with philosophy, not, at least, as philosophy has been practised for the last several centuries. Certainly, when I find myself puzzled or troubled about how I'm living my life, I'm not very likely to turn to Kant or even to Plato. I'm much more likely to turn to art, to fiction, to poetry or to music. Or, yes, to the Bible and its stories about a people's struggles with these same questions.

Part IV

What Is Man?

'How, in such an alien and inhuman world, can so powerless a creature as Man preserve his aspirations untarnished? A strange mystery it is that Nature, omnipotent but blind, in the revolutions of her secular hurryings through the abysses of space, has brought forth at last a child, subject still to her power, but gifted with sight, with knowledge of good and evil, with the capacity of judging all the works of his unthinking Mother. In spite of Death, the mark and seal of the parental control, Man is yet free, during his brief years, to examine, to criticise, to know, and in imagination to create. To him alone, in the world with which he is acquainted, this freedom belongs; and in this lies his superiority to the resistless forces that control his outward life.'

– Bertrand Russell, 'A Free Man's Worship'

Q

❝ *Why do vegetarians propose a different set of rules for non-human animals? After all, humans are animals too. Why is it all right for a lion to kill and eat an antelope when it isn't for a human? Some people answer that 'We do not need to eat meat,' but why does that matter?* **❞**

A

Alexander George: That we don't need to eat meat matters because it means that the harm that we cause to animals by eating them (depriving them of their lives and usually subjecting them to torturous treatment) is something we could avoid. We are, after all, responsible for the avoidable harm that we cause.

And what about the animals? Are they excused *their* eating of other animals because they can't help it? That strikes me as an odd thing to say. Animals can't be held morally accountable; they simply aren't the kinds of creatures that can be morally blamed for what they do. (Which doesn't mean that *we* can't be held accountable for what we do to them.) So, it's weird to talk about their being exculpated by the fact that, say, they are carnivores. Non-human animals simply aren't in need of exculpation: they aren't the kinds of creatures that can be blamed or praised in the first place.

A

Peter Lipton: Animals are not morally accountable: they cannot be morally blameworthy (or praiseworthy). What is harder to explain is why *we* don't have a responsibility to prevent animals from hurting each other. This is an unnatural thought, yet perhaps technically we would have this responsibility, if we could also find an alternative diet for the natural carnivores. But given our own awful treatment of animals, we should perhaps concentrate on getting our own act together first.

Q

66 *I acknowledge that Descartes ranks as one of the most
important and influential thinkers of modern times. But
then why did he believe that non-human animals were not
sentient, and therefore could not suffer or feel pain? How
could such a brilliant person have the misconception that
non-human animals cannot suffer? When inflicting
vivisection or violent harm, the truth is* screaming *at you
in the face! I am boggled.* **99**

A

Nicholas D. Smith: The problem that lies behind your question is a version of what is called the 'problem of other minds'. The problem is that we can only observe behaviour, and behaviour alone may not be decisive evidence of consciousness. The truth, as you put it, is actually not 'screaming at you in the face'. Even Descartes would not have denied that cats will struggle and make loud noises when you begin to cut them open. The screaming, as you put it, is something that happens when cats are vivisected. The question – on which you and Descartes differ – is whether that screaming should be understood as a decisive indicator of whether the cat actually *feels pain*.

Consider even another human being. You witness them

suffering some injury, and they cry out. You *assume* they are feeling pain, and that is *why* they cry out, because when you injure yourself in the same or similar ways, *you* feel pain, and that is what makes *you* cry out. But if you think about it, the *only* pain – indeed, the *only consciousness of any kind* that you ever have or ever will experience is *your own*.

But are analogies of the sort you make with this other human being (she is like me, so when she cries out, it is for the same reason or reasons) really all that reliable? Do you like the taste of liver? If you do, what do you make of people who *hate* it? Are you male? If so, do you really think that females experience things in *exactly the same* way you do? And so on . . . Now, if such questions arise when it comes to other human beings, how much more complex do they become when you are trying to assess the conscious states of non-human animals, whose neurologies and other morphologies, and whose evolutionary histories are in many ways significantly like ours? A famous question, framed years ago in a famous article by Thomas Nagel, is: what is it like to be a bat? Honest answer: haven't a *clue*! Well, then, what makes you so certain that you *know what it is like to be a cat*??? Is it simply inconceivable, or logically impossible, that a being (such as a cat) might not respond to stimuli in ways that look very similar to the ways we respond to them, but in the case of the cat, there is no intervening instance of anything we would recognise as consciousness? That is what Descartes supposed – that cat screaming was just behavioural only, and not related to consciousness. Since consciousness appears not to be directly observable (except in first-person, as it were), your evidence against Descartes's view is not at all compelling.

Of course, I don't think he had any very good evidence that cats *do not* have consciousness, and I myself suppose they do (at least my two cats do . . . well, sort of). But I have tried to show why your case against Descartes is not as easily made as you seemed to suppose.

Q

66 *Is it possible to establish that dogs dream?* **99**

A

Gabriel Segal: The question falls under the general heading of what philosophers call 'the problem of other minds'. As is usually the case in philosophy, the expression 'the problem of' actually covers a variety of interrelated problems. But one aspect of the general problem might roughly be put like this: how is it possible to know what, if anything, is going on in another being's mind?

Philosophers and psychologists have taken a variety of different approaches to the question. One reasonably popular approach says that we can (and, indeed, do) find out about others' minds by deploying a certain kind of psychological theory. The theory posits mental states as the causes of behaviour and other observable phenomena. So, for example, if you see me taking an umbrella with me as I proceed towards the door, you could infer that I believe that it might rain, that I don't want to get wet and that I believe that my having an umbrella about me is a good way to avoid getting wet in the rain. My having such mental states causes my behaviour with the umbrella.

Under this approach, we know about the mental states of

others in the same way as we know about electrons: they are posits of good causal explanations of observable phenomena.

If this is right, then, in general, we won't get 100 per cent certain, knock-down proofs about the contents of other minds. But we can expect to have well-founded, theoretically justified beliefs about them.

In line with this theoretical approach, I'd say that it has already been reasonably well established that dogs dream. Sleeping dogs exhibit a lot of behavioural signs of dreaming: they make running motions, lick their lips, wag their tails, whimper, growl and so on. Dogs exhibit rapid-eye movement (REM) sleep, which in humans is strongly associated with dreaming. And during REM sleep, dogs exhibit heightened brain activity, just as humans do.

The best explanation for all this is that dogs dream.

Q

**If I could produce a perfect copy of a famous work of art,
would it be as valuable as the original?**

A

Mark Crimmins: A *perfect* copy? Wow! That would be an
incredible technical achievement, requiring immensely pre-
cise matches of material composition and construction. The
product of such a vast and unprecedented undertaking (were
it feasible) would probably merit a price higher than any
original artwork.

But suppose, as you might have intended, that such a
process became commonplace and inexpensive: Titians for
the masses. Then of course the original would fetch a pre-
mium over the copies. Why? Because we value artworks not
only for their intrinsic features – their look, their material
constitution – but for their historical features, for their being
the very objects on which the artists exercised their craft. This
is why prints tend to be less valuable than paintings by the
same artist – they're just a bit towards the replica side of
things. Does this make sense, or is it as pointless a pursuit
as . . . saving one of Britney's cigarette butts? I don't know.
But it's not only artworks that normally gain special interest
for being the genuine historical products rather than replicas.

Fossils are like that as well, as might also be the ring given you by your spouse. And your spouse, too, come to think of it.

If you mixed up an original and an indistinguishable copy, the two would have the same value in one sense but not in another. Same: each has the same chance, given what we can know about it, of being the original and being the replica, so there's no basis on which to prefer one to the other. Different: either of the two would surely get a higher price than any *other* replica, and this is because of the higher value placed on the original, and on a chance of acquiring it rather than a replica.

Q

‹‹ Is there no such thing as bad art? ››

A

Mark Crimmins: Sure there's bad art. And to prove it, here's my ASCII picture of a car:

You might wonder whether the term 'art' even applies at all to this, or to anything that we might want to call 'bad art'. That aside, I don't know exactly what you have in mind. Is it that maybe the term 'art' already excludes what someone might have wanted to call 'bad art' – so that 'good art' is redundant? If that's the question, I suppose I think sometimes the term 'art' is used like that. If we say 'a guitar made by Fred is a work of art', we're probably not using 'art' in a way in which it makes sense to add, 'and a very bad work of art at that'. But in plenty of other cases, we don't use 'art' so that 'bad art' makes no sense.

A rather different issue concerns the *objectivity* of evaluations of artworks. If I say 'that drawing is really bad', does the word 'bad' denote, once and for all, an objective category of artworks, so that my statement is true or false depending on whether the drawing falls in that category? Or does my statement do only a more *subjective* job, perhaps of expressing *my* distaste for the drawing? Or is it somewhere in between those extremes – maybe asserting that the drawing would be regarded as distasteful by people of a certain type (perhaps, people to whose tastes in art I accord a certain kind of respect)?

That philosophers have studied these (and many other) options as to what 'bad' means in this kind of statement is a consequence of what can seem a rather odd tension: on the one hand, we talk simply in terms of 'good/bad' rather than 'good to me/bad to me' or the like; and this makes it sound like we take it to be an objective matter of fact what's good or bad. On the other hand it seems clear that our judgments about what artworks are good or bad are guided by our own tastes and reactions; this makes it seem like we must *really* be expressing something about our own idiosyncratic evaluations rather than about an objective measure. In this respect, 'that's a good drawing' seems intermediate between 'that's a good flavour of ice-cream' (which seems quite subjective), and 'that's a good knife-sharpener' (which seems considerably more objective). Part of the difference here may be that whereas it's silly to argue about whether vanilla ice-cream is good, or to ask for reasons for thinking so, that's not true in the case of the knife-sharpener.

Is it silly to argue and reason about whether an artwork is good or bad? Certainly it's an extremely common practice – could it really be as silly as arguing about chocolate versus vanilla? Suppose it does in fact make sense; does that show that 'good/bad', as applied to artworks, marks once and for all an objective distinction? Or does argument and reasoning merely reflect optimism that we're not so different in our evaluative dispositions, so that disagreement about what's good or bad art might well only reflect differences in factual knowledge and in sorting matters out – differences that can be remedied though discussion?

The distinctions and issues here are of great interest especially insofar as they illuminate two other sorts of evaluative talk that are Big Game philosophically: moral and rational evaluation.

Q

66 When we read stories in a book, do the characters actually come to life? Are they in some sense real, or do they actually believe they are real?

How do I know that my life is real and that I'm not some fictional creation of someone's mind? 99

A

Mark Crimmins: When you consider that characters in stories are so much like us, it can be disconcerting: if they're like us, then we're like them, too. Indeed, what distinguishes us? Just that they're in stories and we're in reality? But couldn't they say the same about us?

That's a very tempting line of thought, but we should resist it.

There is a big difference between something's being represented as being so, and its being so. I can *say* that I have fixed the car, but that doesn't make it true that I've fixed the car. Someone might counter, yes it does – it makes it true *according to you.* But being true according to me is not a *way* of being true any more than being *not* true is a way of being true. This can be a little hard to see because of a very natural way we have of describing what someone has said. Often, instead of saying, 'Crimmins says that the car is fixed,' we say, 'The car is fixed, according to Crimmins.' That makes it sound like the car *is* fixed, though not in reality but only in the according-to-Crimmins reality. But really it's just a picturesque way of saying the same thing, namely, that I have said something that represents the car as having been fixed.

The same is true in our talk about fictions. Instead of saying, 'Conan Doyle, in the *Holmes* stories, represented that there was a detective named "Holmes" who was very smart,' we say, 'Holmes was a very smart detective, in Conan Doyle's *Holmes* stories,' or even just 'Holmes was a very smart detective.' That makes it sound like there really was this detective, just not in reality. But, again, that's a mistake that arises from a picturesque style of describing what is represented (in this case, in fiction) as being so. A feature of fictional characters that is puzzling if you think they are 'real but not in reality' is called *fictional incompleteness*: did Holmes ever have a bunion on his left big toe? It's not just that we don't *know* – there's no fact of the matter, because all the 'facts about Holmes' are settled by the stories, and it's unsettled there. This is no mystery at all if we realise that the only genuine facts are that the stories *represent* various things as being the case (but quite a mystery if Holmes is as real as we are).

Q

66 *Is music a language?* **99**

A

Mark Sprevak: There is no uncontroversial definition of a language. However, a requirement that is often cited is that there should be rules on how different elements of a language are composed together (syntax). Another requirement is that the elements of a language should have representational content (semantics).

Music arguably passes the first requirement: notes cannot be strung together in any way one likes to make music. But it appears to fail the second requirement: it is not obvious that individual musical notes represent anything at all. One might argue that sometimes there are phrases in music that do represent: for example, different instrumental lines in Prokofiev's *Peter and the Wolf* represent the activities of different animals. But these tend to be rather isolated cases of representation; they are not as widespread and systematic as one would expect from a language (e.g., flutes in music do not always represent birds, or indeed anything at all).

Even if music is not a language in the above sense, that

does not mean that there aren't interesting connections between language and music, or that our linguistic and musical abilities aren't related.

Q

66 *If there were a theory of everything, wouldn't it predict all human action and behaviour? And so wouldn't this theory destroy the possibility of free will?* **99**

A

Peter Lipton: This is an excellent question, and philosophers do not all answer it in the same way. My own view is that predictability in itself is not a special threat to free will. Suppose that I have free will. Now suppose that you know me so well that you can predict every move I will make. So long as you don't use that information to influence me, but just know it, I don't think that takes away my free will, because you are not interfering.

One of the things that makes this question difficult is that we have trouble seeing how free will is ever possible, prediction or not. The classic dilemma is this: either everything has a cause or not. If everything does have a cause, then it looks like you have no free will, because the chain of causes leading to your actions began before you were born. And if not everything has a cause, if in particular some of your actions are uncaused, then that doesn't seem like free will either. It seems just like a random event. In short, either determinism is true or it isn't; if determinism is true you have no free will; if determinism is not true you have no free will; so you just don't have free will. Philosophers have worked long and hard to try to show what is wrong with this argument, but it's a tough nut to crack.

The good news about free will is that our actions having external causes is entirely compatible with their also having internal causes, in the form of our beliefs and desires. My consumption of a banana split was caused in part by the presence of that item on the menu – an external cause – but also by a desire on my part. If I had not had that desire, or if my desire to lose weight had been stronger, I would not have eaten the banana split. So insofar as the existence of internal causes is enough for us to grant someone free will, then the existence of external causes is compatible with free will, since the existence of external causes is compatible with the existence of internal causes.

In ordinary life, when we think someone did it because he wanted to, we think he did it of his own free will. Unfortunately, when we start thinking more abstractly about the meaning of free will, it starts to seem that the fact that he did it because he wanted to isn't enough for free will, and we cannot seem to come up with what one could possibly add that would make it enough.

Q

66 *I believe that all human actions are born of self-interest:
even so-called selfless acts are committed in order to
assuage guilt, or to obtain approval from others, or even to
get that good feeling you get when you know you have
done a good deed (which is essentially selfish, considering
that you get a mental reward, instead of a material one).
How can you disagree?* **99**

A

Peter Lipton: A powerful demon gave me a choice at lunch
the other day: either my children will thrive and I will think
they are miserable (which will make me feel miserable), or my
children will really be miserable but I will think they are
thriving (which will make me feel very happy). The moment
after I choose, I will have no memory of having made a choice
or indeed of having ever had lunch with a demon. You know
what? I'm going to choose happy children and miserable me.
I'm no angel, but that is a selfless act.

A

Jyl Gentzler: The fact that we usually feel pleasure after we
are aware of having performed an act that we believe is

good does not imply that we performed the good act for the sake of the pleasure we expected to feel when we succeeded. True: we do *many* things simply for the sake of the pleasure that they allow us to feel. Many people, much of the time, have sex simply because they enjoy doing so, and if they didn't enjoy sex, they wouldn't, and perhaps couldn't, have sex. But not all actions are like that. We do some of the things that we do simply because we think that they're worthwhile. Since we believe that they're worthwhile, we will feel satisfaction upon learning that we accomplished something worthwhile. However, it can't be the case that we performed these acts for the sake of the pleasure that our success causes, since our feeling this pleasure in the first place depends on our giving independent value to these acts or the consequences of these acts. For example, if I didn't think that it was a good idea to contribute some of my limited resources to Oxfam, then I wouldn't feel pleasure at my act of doing so. So my believing that it's a good idea for me to contribute to Oxfam can't be due simply to my expectation that I will experience pleasure at the thought of having done so.

A

Thomas Pogge: Given the great diversity of human conduct across epochs and cultures, it is easy to find plausible counter-examples. But such counter-examples can always be rebuffed by a remark such as the one you have provided: the act appears to be selfless, but was really motivated by the satisfaction the agent expected to derive from assuaging his guilt or from the approval by others. Even when a person throws himself on a hand grenade to save his comrades, one can say that the expected satisfaction from the anticipated approval of his comrades must have outweighed his dread of the anticipated pain and death.

The problem with such rebuffs is that they lead to circularity: The fact that a person acted in a certain way is taken as sufficient to show that he must have had some selfish motive for doing so. And the proposition in question (that all human actions are born of self-interest) then becomes entirely immune to refutation. You repeat it no matter what actions are performed. And then it no longer expresses a (disturbing) discovery about the particular world we live in.

To demonstrate this, take another proposition: *people always do what they prefer*. This proposition is harmless and trivial when preference and choice are conceptually linked so that an agent's preferred conduct option is, by definition, the one she chooses. Or consider the proposition: *every person is directly motivated only by desires that are her own*. This again is not a psychological discovery but a harmless conceptual truth: another's desire can motivate me only indirectly, when I know about it and desire that it be fulfilled.

To explore your own understanding of the proposition in question (that all human actions are born of self-interest), ask yourself what you would count as good evidence for a genuinely altruistic act. If you find, on reflection, that you would count no conceivable conduct as such good evidence, then your proposition is independent of what human beings do and are like, and hence not informative about them. If, on the other hand, you find that you recognise the possibility of conduct that you would count as good evidence for non-selfish motives, then you are likely to find such actual conduct in the world – though you may also conclude, as Immanuel Kant did, that it is never *certain* that a person's conduct is not selfishly motivated.

Q

66 *If determinism were true, so every action was fixed from the beginning of the universe by the laws of nature, would this undermine morality? Would Hitler be morally equivalent to Gandhi because both were determined to act the way they did? Should this affect the anger we feel towards 'immoral' people?* **99**

A

Peter Lipton: This is a big question, but I will just tell a story familiar to philosophers working in this area. A man is found guilty of a crime, and is allowed to give a brief speech before sentencing. He admits the crime, but claims not only to be a criminal but also a philosopher, and one who has convinced himself of the truth of determinism. Since everything he did was determined by causes before he was born, he could not have done otherwise but commit the crime. So surely he should not be punished. The judge, having listened carefully to all this, admits that she too has a sideline in philosophy, and that she too is a determinist. So she cannot help but punish him.

When we consider the relationship between determinism and responsibility, we have a tendency not to be entirely consistent. Thus we may think that we should not punish criminals nor feel anger towards them. But what is the force of this 'should not' if we too are determined? We just do what we are determined to do. Since we could not do otherwise, 'should' and 'should not' do not seem to come into it.

Q

66 *Do people need speech in order to think?* **99**

A

Louise Antony: You probably have experienced the following phenomenon: there's a word or a name that you are trying to remember, but you just can't. It seems to 'be there', somehow, just out of reach, or just out of sight. It is, as we sometimes say, 'right on the tip of my tongue'. If you do any writing, you have probably experienced a more substantial version of this: you feel like you know *what* you want to say, but you just 'can't find the right words' to say it.

Everyday experiences like these suggest that thought is something separate from speech, that speech is 'externalised thought'. Many philosophers, however, hold that this appearance is misleading. These philosophers – and they are probably in the majority – hold that thought and language are essentially tied together, so that there cannot be one without the other. (Leave aside all the evidence from casual observation that it's all too possible to talk without thinking.) The argument for this view appeals to the evidence we usually need for attributing thoughts to others, namely, verbal behaviour. There is also the consideration you raise, that thinking sort of 'feels' like talking silently to oneself.

The inconvenient thing about this view is that it requires us to deny that pre-verbal children and animals have thought. And while we don't have exactly the same evidence for attributing thought to such beings as we have in the case of fully verbal adults, we do nonetheless have *lots* of evidence that such beings think. Indeed, the best accounts available of how children *acquire* language requires us to attribute thoughts to them – at a minimum, thoughts like 'So *that*'s what that thing is called . . .'. Also, most philosophers believe that the emergence of language involves the emergence of *conventions* – unstated mutual agreements that certain things will be done in certain ways, that we'll use 'dog' to refer to dogs. But conventions require, not only *thinking*, but *thinking about thinking*. To participate in a convention, I must not only grasp that a certain sound made by another human being is correlated with the presence of dogs, I must grasp that that person *intends* to *communicate to me* the presence of a dog.

Then, too, a great deal depends on what one means by 'thinking'.

Philosophers in the second group contend that thinking only involves having and manipulating *representations* of the world, so that we're justified in attributing thought to a creature if we have to posit representations in order to explain the creature's behaviour. We know, for example, that chimpanzees can find novel solutions to problems: left alone in a room with a box and a banana dangling above them, just out of their reach, they figure out to move the box below the banana and climb on to it. This cannot be simply a conditioned response; the chimps have had no experience with standing on boxes before. So we have to assume that they somehow represented to themselves a situation that did not yet exist, and that they went through some process of reasoning to get it, like: 'If I were taller, I could reach the banana. If I stood on that box, I'd be taller. Hence, I should try to stand on that box.' But now you're going to ask, 'How could the chimp think that if it doesn't have the words to express it?' Answer: the chimp thinks in a kind of 'private' language – a built-in system of representation. If this seems implausible, try giving an alternative explanation of the chimp's accomplishment, one that doesn't end up making the same assumption.

Philosophers in the first camp, who think there can be no thought without language, may just mean by 'thought' something that is consciously accessible, something that one can reflect about. Perhaps this kind of 'self-conscious' thought really *is* tied necessarily to language. Some of these philosophers then allow that animals and pre-verbal human children can have 'thought-like states' that play the same role in explaining behaviour as do the 'mental representations' posited by the cognitive scientists. But in that case the issue becomes merely verbal, and merely verbal issues are boring.

Q

« How do words get their meaning? »

A

Mark Crimmins: Well, there's a panel of very wise elders who meet in an oaken room in their black robes and officially confer meaning on words. At least, that's the idea you'd get the way some people talk about 'correct' meanings, as they bemoan the fact that most people nowadays use the 'wrong' ones. Linguists find this funny, because words simply mean what people use them to mean. The linguistic-correctness freak wrongly assumes that fussy usage manuals and out-dated dictionaries determine the 'correct' meaning of words, when the real tribunal is ordinary use. So 'meat' comes to mean edible flesh rather than food in general not because of a dictionary change but because of a shift in ordinary usage. Dictionaries respond to changes in usage; they don't mandate them.

How exactly does ordinary use manage to create linguistic meaning? The philosopher Paul Grice developed a very influential answer to this question. His idea is that the fundamental kind of 'meaning' isn't *linguistic* meaning, but *communicative* meaning. A person can 'mean something' in the sense of trying to get a message across to another – they can wink, ring a bell or, of course, use language, with the open intent of getting some message across. Grice suggested that what gives words meaning is that they become standardised as tools for getting certain sorts of messages across. What they mean is a matter of what messages they standardly help to convey. And this is a question of how words are actually used rather than how they are defined in reference books.

This all seems very insightful and important. But maybe the linguistic-correctness freak isn't entirely mistaken. There certainly is a sizeable linguistic community whose members treat dictionaries and usage manuals as norms to be lived up to (whether or not they capture ordinary usage). By these language users' own lights, they speak incorrectly when the 'experts' say so; they hold themselves to the experts' rules. With respect to this community, it may well be plausible to say that their words literally mean what the usage mavens deem them to mean. Does this mean that Grice is wrong about them? Maybe so. And not just about the linguistically correct. If the idea becomes common that General Relativity is the claim that 'everything is relative', people will use the term to convey messages about everything being relative. But surely this would be a widespread *mistake* about what 'General Relativity' means; it wouldn't become *correct*. So perhaps Grice's theory needs supplementation to accommodate cases in which language users *defer* to experts to settle literal meaning.

Q

*" A married man and an unmarried woman are on the verge
of involvement. Does the woman have a responsibility to
protect the man's marriage vows, or is the responsibility
solely his? In the absence of any specific religious doctrine,
how would you frame a principle to help determine where
the responsibility begins and ends here? "*

A

David Brink: You don't have to be religious to think that trust
and fidelity are important values that should regulate inti-
mate associations. So, barring some special background that
you have not supplied (e.g. the marriage is an 'open marriage'
or the wife has been in a persistent vegetative state for years),
I would think that the extramarital affair was morally wrong,
at least in part because it was inconsistent with marital trust
and fidelity. It seems to me the unmarried woman does wrong
if she knowingly enters such a relationship, even if it is not
her own vows that are being broken. If it's wrong for you to
breach a contract, and if I knowingly help you breach your
contract, I've done something wrong. Moreover, if the
unmarried woman genuinely cares for the married man, then
she presumably has reason not to want him to do something
wrong. At least, this sort of moralised concern for another is a

feature of other forms of love, such as parental love for a child. So, to answer your original question, this concern gives her reason not to contribute to his infidelity. But this concern seems to be an additional reason not to have the affair, in addition to the primary reason not to facilitate infidelity.

A

Matthew Silverstein: When I read your description of the situation, my first thought was that the unmarried woman has a responsibility not to protect the married man's *vows*, but rather to protect the married man's *wife*. After all, his wife is the one who is most likely to be harmed by her husband's affair, and we all have a responsibility not to act in ways that are likely to cause harm to others (even if we don't personally know the others in question). Of course, it is the man who bears the brunt of the responsibility in this case, since he has a specific obligation to care for his wife. Nonetheless, I do think that the woman is at least partly responsible for the negative consequences of her affair.

Q

66 *Am I morally bound to tell my sex partner if I fantasise about someone else while making love to her? Or to disclose the subject of the fantasy for that matter?* **99**

A

Thomas Pogge: Suppose you were indeed morally obligated to tell your sex partner when you fantasise about someone else while making love to her. This obligation would not be one owed to any third party. So it would have to be one you owe to her. But it is questionable that lovers owe one another such disclosures. Are you convinced that your partner has a duty to disclose any fantasies she may have to you? Would such disclosures be in your interest? Would you want to know what she fantasises about when the two of you make love? Would you be happier if she gave you this information, or do you think she would be happier if she gave it to you? If the answers to these empirical questions are negative, then it is hard to see how she could owe you such disclosures that you would not want and that would be of no benefit to either of you. And then you should assume that you don't owe her such disclosures either – unless you have special reason to believe that she would want them or that she or you would benefit from them.

A

Jyl Gentzler: Many people feel duty-bound to reveal every wayward thought to their partners. Speaking only personally, if I were your partner, I would very much prefer not to know. While I am confident that it would not reflect badly on me to learn that you fantasise about sex with someone else (after all, hasn't everyone, no matter how stellar their relationship, thought, however briefly, about sex with someone else?), I'm not sure that I would be so mature and rational as to not drive myself (and you) crazy by getting fixated on the particularities of the fantasy. Why her? What does she have that I don't have? And so on.

You might think that our relationship would be better if nothing were hidden between us and that I would be a better person if I overcame the irrationality and immaturity that would prevent me from imagining your sexual fantasies with equanimity. If you truly cared about me and our relationship, you might think, you would tell me the truth so that both our relationship and I would have an opportunity to grow. However, it just might be the case that I *cannot* grow in this way, and that consequently the only effects of your revelation would be harms to me and to our relationship.

Further, I'm not convinced that we should hold up as a romantic ideal a relationship in which the partners' mental lives are transparent to one another. While one great benefit of intimacy is the opportunity to share, without fear of rejection, anger or revulsion, thoughts and desires that are not proper topics of more public conversations, it remains the case that much that goes on in our messy minds is not fit for *any* conversation. Thoughts and desires that are articulated have to be responded to – either explicitly accepted or rejected, or blatantly ignored. But why should I impose on others (especially beloved others) the demand to respond to thoughts or desires that I myself regard as wayward, random, unjustifiable or boring?

Q

❝ *Is it possible for one to be in love with the feeling of being in love, instead of with the person you believe you're in love with?* **❞**

A

Alexander George: We do speak of 'loving the feeling of being clean', but surely the sense of 'loving' here must be different from the sense in which one loves one's spouse. The first seems more or less synonymous with 'finding very pleasurable', while the latter – well, I don't know how else to express what we mean in such cases, but I do know that we mean something different from 'finding very pleasurable' (which is of course compatible with saying that loving someone can be very pleasurable). So, it's of course quite possible that John is in love with Hilary and also finds being in that state very pleasurable.

But that's not quite your question. You're imagining a situation in which John *thinks* he's in love with Hilary, but really isn't. (People do speak as if they can be wrong about whether they are in love: 'I thought I loved him, but now I realise I never did.' That's interesting in itself and perhaps offers some clues about how, and how not, to treat the notion of love.) And you're further wondering whether John might experience great pleasure from this *faux* love. If he does, then of course he's not in love with being in love – since he's *not* in love. As you put it, he's 'in love with *the feeling* of being in love'.

Putting it this way does assume that love *feels* a particular way. This seems like a dubious assumption to me (recall that one can think one's in love when one isn't), but if we do assume it then your question amounts to this: could it be that John is not in love with Hilary, that John is having those experiences that regularly attend his being in love, that (perhaps as a consequence) John believes that he is in love with Hilary, and finally that John is taking great pleasure in having those experiences? I don't see why not.

Q

66 *I really love my wife and of course I never want to hurt her. But is it moral to cheat on her if I'm 100 per cent sure that she won't know (and therefore won't be hurt)?* **99**

A

Alexander George: I don't see how one could be '100 per cent sure'. Maybe, just maybe, there are some claims about the natural world of which one could be absolutely certain, like the fact that one was born to parents and didn't grow on a tree. But I don't think most claims about the future are ones we can be so certain of, and surely not a claim like 'My wife will never discover that I cheated on her.'

But if you want to take a case where we can be confident that the person cheated on will never discover the betrayal, let's imagine that your wife asked you to promise her that you will never have sexual relations with another person even after she, your wife, has passed away. You do so promise her and now she has passed away. Clearly, we can be '100 per cent sure' in this case that your wife will never be hurt by your 'cheating' on her. (I'm obviously assuming here that she won't be pained in some afterlife.) Would it be immoral to break your promise in these circumstances?

Some will say that it wouldn't be, that thinking so is a

habit-induced illusion. On this view, one can only wrong someone by doing something that causes her pain. Others would insist that it would be wrong in these circumstances to break your promise, that talking of right and wrong isn't merely a shorthand for talking about what would hurt a person. On this view, that would be to get things backwards: the wrongness of your actions doesn't consist in your having hurt her. Rather, the reason your wife would have been hurt had she discovered your infidelity is that she would have learned *that you had wronged her*, and *that* is what would be painful.

Q

66 *Given the complexity of human relations, it seems almost inevitable that a normal human will have more than one partner during his/her lifetime. Have we therefore entered an age where 'I love you' has been devalued from the 'I love you for ever' of our forefathers to merely 'I love you at the moment'? Is it possible to love two people at once?* 99

A

Nicholas D. Smith: I guess I want to begin by saying that I deny your premise. I think we actually have very little reason for thinking that our forefathers were more loving, or meant more when they said 'I love you' than we do. It may be true that marriages did not as often end in divorce as they do now, but I strongly suspect that the explanations of this fact have very little to do with our ancestors being more loving, or more stable in their loves. In many ways, actually, I am inclined to think that the relevant sorts of relationships in most cultures of earlier times were more exploitative, more limiting, more unequal, and less about 'love' (in any form I would be willing to recognise) than relationships are now, at least where women's rights are recognised (if not, alas, always respected).

As for your second question, the answer will depend upon what you mean by 'love'. Certainly most people who love their spouses also love their children, parents and close friends. But you would no doubt object that these are different *kinds* of love. I have a suspicion that absolutely *every* attachment that goes by the name of 'love' is in some ways different in kind from every other such attachment, and so in some sense it will be true that one won't have the very same feelings for any two people at once or even in an entire lifetime. But perhaps you would still find this an evasion of your question. Perhaps you mean by 'love' a kind of attachment that is absolutely exclusive of any others of the same kind. (But if that's your definition, then the answer to your question immediately follows.) It *may* be (though I tend to doubt it) that there is a kind (or are kinds) of love that is (are) completely exclusive, but most kinds of love, obviously, are not exclusive in that way. Romantic love seems to *tend* to exclusivity – but I think many people have found themselves in a situation where they would honestly claim to love more than one person romantically. One thing is for sure in such cases, given the way society is configured: such a person's life is likely to become *very* complicated!

Q

66 *What's it like to be another person?* **99**

A

Mark Crimmins: That's a really good question. I guess the answer is: it feels normal. Because it feels normal to them, and so if you *are* that person, then feeling like they do feels normal to you.

But what we really want to know is: how would it feel for *me* to feel what they are feeling? If I could 'see' what a red apple looked like to them, would it look red to me? Or would it look green? If I could feel their sleepiness, would it feel like mine? Fortunately, philosophers have thought long and hard about this question. Unfortunately, we haven't figured it out yet.

Q

&& *Do we have any control over what we believe? I can think of countless things that I hold to be true that for all the tea in China I couldn't make myself think otherwise. When we're presented with good grounds for believing something, is it possible to not believe it? Do we have any choice on the matter? I realise that some people can enter a state of denial over something, but isn't this just acting as if they didn't hold that particular belief? Is it possible in theory to be caused (perhaps through hypnosis or indoctrination) to believe or not believe something contrary to what would normally seem obvious to us?* **&&**

A

Mitchell S. Green: Belief is Janus-faced. Viewed from one side, beliefs seem to happen to us, and to do so in a way that depends on what evidence is available: Faced with sensory evidence of a charging rhino, it's virtually impossible not to believe that a rhino is charging. Viewed from another angle, however, beliefs seem at least in part to be subject to our will. This is suggested by the fact that I might say to my audience, 'Believe me', as a preface to what I am about to say, and they might well reply, 'I find it hard to believe that!'

One impetus for the second theme, where belief seems to

some degree subject to our will, is the 'Wager' argument of the philosopher/mathematician Blaise Pascal (1623–1662). Pascal held that it is not possible to prove that God exists, and not possible to prove that God does not exist. He argued that nevertheless it is in one's best interest to believe that God exists. How, then, can one cultivate a belief in God in the absence of proof? Pascal's answer was that if you surround yourself with religious people, go to church (or the mosque, or synagogue, etc.) for long enough, listen to the right kind of music, etc., then eventually belief will come. Similarly, if I want (perhaps because someone will pay me a lot of money if I do so) to bring it about that I believe that Greenland is not melting, I could hire hypnotists, ask friends to make sure I don't see newspaper articles discussing global warming, hang out with people who deny the phenomenon of global warming, and so on. It seems likely that after a while, belief (in the proposition that Greenland is not melting) will 'come to stupefy my scruples', to borrow a phrase from William James's famous essay, 'The Will to Believe'. (See his *The Will to Believe and Other Essays in Popular Philosophy*, Longmans, Green and Co., 1989). Notice, though, that in both these cases, the agent modifying her beliefs needs to suppress contrary evidence. As a result, I would suggest that it is possible to believe something contrary to what would seem obvious, but only if the obvious counter-evidence has fallen out of view. With the rhino still charging, no way.

Most philosophers would agree that it is possible to modify one's beliefs at will, given enough time and determination. Most, however, would also agree that it is impossible to believe something at will 'just like that', that is, simply as a result of deciding to do so. However, two questions arise from this distinction between forming beliefs directly and forming them indirectly.

1. If it is indeed impossible to form beliefs indirectly, why is that? Many would suggest that this is due to the mechanism by which beliefs are formed, depending in many ways on perception which does not seem subject to our control. However, many of our beliefs are formed in non-perceptual ways – so shouldn't we be able to form such beliefs at will? More generally, is the alleged impossibility of directly forming beliefs at will a conceptual impossibility (like finding a married bachelor) or an impossibility relative to human psychology (like, for most of us, memorising a phone book)?

2. Do we have a solid grasp on the distinction itself? I borrowed the phrase 'just like that' from Bernard Williams's well-known essay, 'Deciding to Believe' (from his book, *Problems of the Self*, Cambridge University Press, 1973), but one might have doubts that it marks out a clear phenomenon. Suppose for instance that I am considering an issue on which there is evidence going both ways – say the thesis that a certain drug reduces the risk of cancer. It seems that after a while I might decide that the drug is effective. However, I could do that without gathering *more* data; rather, this is a conclusion I might reach after careful consideration of the data I already had. Is this a case of deciding to believe 'just like that'?

Q

Is it possible that people who are mentally unstable (a little on the crazy side) are actually sane and that we are the crazy ones?

A

Richard Heck: Suppose that, as you walked into your office building, you found people screaming and running in all directions. Security guards accosted you and dragged you out. So you walked home, found your key didn't work, knocked on the door, and a stranger answered! You asked them what they were doing there, and they said they lived there and were wondering what *you* were doing there. Next thing you knew, the men in white coats had arrived, and things just went downhill from there. You might reasonably start thinking you're crazy. But are you? Or is it the world that has gone crazy?

The notion of 'sanity' is, in one way or another, a notion of normal mental functioning. But there are two very different notions of normality. One such notion is a statistical one: what is 'normal' is simply what is common (or average, or what have you) in a given population. Another notion is normative: what is normal is what is proper, in accord with the rules, and the like.

The contrast between these two notions emerges in different ways in different cases, but the contrast can usually be uncovered by considering modal statements. Would what is now normal *still* be normal if things were very different from how they now are? For example, it is normal for human beings to have five fingers on each hand. Suppose genetically modified corn carried some kind of virus so that, if a pregnant woman were to eat it, her children would have six fingers on each hand. Suppose further that such corn becomes very common, so that babies everywhere start to be born with twelve fingers. No one knows what the cause is, so this continues for a long time, until most everyone has twelve fingers. Is it then 'normal' for humans to have twelve fingers? If you're inclined to say 'yes', then you are using a purely statistical notion of what is normal; if you're inclined to say 'no', then you are using a normative one.

Of course, since everything in philosophy is controversial, there are philosophers who deny that there is any non-statistical notion of normality. They're wrong. In fact, I think the more important sense of 'normal' is the normative one. So let me now use the word 'usual' to mean 'normal', in the statistical sense, leaving the word 'normal' ambiguous.

With all of that said, we can now ask: is it possible that people who are mentally unusual are actually the ones who are normal? No, if the notion of normality is statistical; yes, if the notion of normality is normative. That is, it's possible, in the minimal sense that it's conceivable; we can't simply rule it out *a priori*. Maybe, as with the previous example, there is some environmental factor (say, reality television) that has

caused most people not to have the kind of mental functioning they should have.

Whether that is in fact so is, of course, not a question for
philosophers.

Q

66 *Recently, a friend had an operation in which she was given medication to make her forget the operation: it was an eye operation done under local anaesthetic, and apparently the 'scalpel coming at your eye' memory causes nightmare reactions. So, she must have had an instant of terror on seeing the scalpel cutting into her eye, but now has no recall. If so, was she really ever terrified? If there is no memory of it whatsoever, can we call it 'terror'? If so, how do any of us know that we haven't been similarly terrified?* 99

A

Amy Kind: Let's assume that if your friend had not been given the amnesic medicine, we would agree that she experienced terror when the scalpel approached her eye. The question then becomes: why should the administration of the amnesic medicine change our view?

Given your description of the medicine – that it 'makes her forget the operation' – it does not prevent her from having experiences; it just causes her to forget those experiences. So, to answer your question, yes, she was terrified. She had an experience of terror, and she is now unable to recall that experience.

You seem to be assuming that we must be able to remember an experience in order for it to have been truly experienced. I am inclined to deny this assumption. To help see why we should deny the assumption, consider a slightly different case. Suppose someone has an instant of terror and then dies. Would you want to deny that she experienced the terror, even though (due to her death) she never was able to form a memory of the terror?

Q

66 *Many years ago someone asked a question I'm still unable to answer. While in Pakistan, I met a co-worker's wife. We got along very well and had a great time discussing something we both enjoyed very much: cooking. At one point, she turned to me and asked, 'What does an avocado taste like?' They just weren't available to her in Lahore. She had seen pictures and read recipes but had never had one. I couldn't relate the taste through comparison because avocados are unique. How do you express or talk about flavour without a base to compare it with? How can someone share perception without a common experience?* 99

A

Joseph G. Moore: That's a great question, and a great example. There are several obstacles to conveying the taste of an avocado to another person in words. Some are practical, and some philosophical.

I bet I could reliably distinguish avocados from other substances in a blind taste-test, but if I'm not currently eating the avocado, describing the taste becomes much more diffi-cult. Even now that I'm eating an avocado (honestly), my powers of discrimination seem much greater than my woeful powers of description. Here goes: avocados have a buttery (but harder and more oily), earthen flavour, similar to a non-stringy mango, but less sweet . . . OK, agreed – this description would be much better if I were a gourmet or a poet, and not a clunky philosopher. But even so, some have argued that the felt qualities of our sensations are *ineffable* – the way things taste to us (as well as how they look, sound, smell and feel) will always elude our most sensitive, evocative and fine-grained descriptions.

What this really means, and whether this is so, are matters of debate. But it's clear that we're hampered in any case by our lack of a 'purely qualitative' language for picking out the way things taste to us. By this I mean that most of our taste-descriptions invariably make reference to some external substance (or type of substance), and then say, in effect, that the current taste is similar to that typically caused by the substance. When we describe a food as salty, for example, we mean that it tastes the way things with salt in them taste (even if the food in question contains no salt). If this is right, then your friend will have to have tasted the substances (like mangoes) that are invoked in describing the taste of an avocado. And even this won't suffice if the taste is, as you suggest, unique – if it can't be experienced as built up out of other tastes. (This may or may not be true of avocados, but I doubt it is true of all tastes: I think you can reasonably know the taste of chocolate-flavoured coffee if you've tasted chocolate and coffee.) These points about the way we describe tastes, and the difficulties we confront in conveying them, lead directly to two philosophical questions that are fraught and fascinating.

First, we might wonder whether there really is a stable 'way that an avocado tastes' for us to describe, since taste discriminations vary across people (and also within each one of us across time). But even if you and your friend discriminate tastes in just the same way, there's always the worry that in principle your tastes could be systematically reversed: perhaps the things that taste salty to you taste sweet to her (even though she calls them 'salty') and vice versa. Philosophers have thought long, hard and inconclusively about whether this possibility can be squared with the materialist view that tastes are no more than physical states of the brain. In fact, some argue that this type of inversion isn't genuinely possible because there isn't really any private avocado-taste that we introspect or examine with some inner-eye of consciousness.

Second, your example gives rise to one of the most famous and controversial thought experiments in contemporary philosophy. This comes from the Australian philosopher, Frank Jackson, and it supports the opposing view – that our inner taste sensations are not only very real, but non-physical at that! I'll modify the argument to your example. Suppose your friend goes back to school, and without ever tasting an avocado, becomes the world's leading expert on the psychology and neurophysiology of taste, as well as on the chemistry of avocados. One day she tastes her first avocado and exclaims: 'Aha, *that's* what an avocado tastes like!' It seems that your friend has come to learn a non-physical fact, since she already knew all those that the physical sciences could teach her. According to this argument, your inability to convey the taste of an avocado to your friend reflects not only practical difficulties and limitations of our language, but also the fact that tastes are not physical!

Q

66 *When I encounter a rock, is there a two-way flow of information between me and the rock? Information about the rock is sent to me via my senses. Is there a reciprocal flow of information from me to the rock?* 99

A

Mark Crimmins: In perception, you are affected by the rock. You are changed, and the rock is the cause of the changes. Change means that you acquire some different properties. Now, some of your properties are *intrinsic* and some *extrinsic*. Philosophers have a hell of a time trying to explain that distinction clearly, but, roughly, an intrinsic property of something has to do purely with the situation 'inside' it as opposed to elsewhere. Since your conscious states, and other sensory and cognitive states, are changed, you have undergone intrinsic change, and, as you say, your new intrinsic states bear information about the rock in virtue of its having caused them.

Now, the rock is also changed intrinsically by the encounter. Your gravitational attraction affects it some, and light bouncing off you hits the rock and changes it in various slight ways.

Unlike you, however, the rock is unable to collect and decipher the traces of your presence that impact it, and so your effects upon the rock's intrinsic properties are subtle and diffuse. However, the encounter has also changed some *extrinsic* properties of the rock: it now has the properties of being perceived, of being thought interesting, and so on. The rock has no clue of this, but in fact you have elevated it into participation in the world of thought.

Q

66 *If you watch a car drive away, it appears to get smaller. We know that it doesn't really get smaller, it only appears to get smaller. So we distinguish between the real size of the car and its apparent size. The real car is outside our heads, and the apparent car is an image of the real car and so inside our heads. But then what we actually see is both outside our heads and inside our heads – but how can it be both?* 99

A

Joseph G. Moore: There are interesting tensions here, I agree, but they reside in the way that we talk about appearances rather than in the distinction between appearance and reality itself.

Size is an *intrinsic* property – that is, a car's size, like its shape, depends entirely upon the way it alone is, and not upon the ways it's contingently related to other things around it. Apparent-size, by contrast, is a relational or *extrinsic* property, and subtly so: a car's apparent-size depends not just upon the car's real size, but also upon the relative location of the relevant viewer. Thus, the car's apparent-size to Fred can shrink if the car shrinks in size, but also (and using less magic) if Fred and the car move apart so that light from the car takes up a smaller portion in Fred's visual field. So, one and the same car can consistently maintain its real size and change its apparent-size through changes only in the relative position of the viewer.

Our judgment of a car's apparent-size seems to come straight from our perception of the car alone. My own position as a viewer isn't an explicit part of the scene that's presented to me visually. (I don't typically see myself seeing something as I see it.) And so, apparent-size may present itself to me from the inside as if it were an intrinsic property of the car I see. But it isn't.

This gives rise to your worry: the only type of size a real car has is the type that doesn't generally change when it drives away; but there's another type of size, apparent-size, that does change; and so, there must be something other than a real car – perhaps a 'mental car' or an image of the car – that undergoes a change in this second type of size. But here's where we need to remind ourselves that the real car can consistently undergo a change in apparent-size without a change in real size if there's been a change in its distance from the viewer. There's no inconsistency here, and so no need for a suspect second type of car. This is no different from the way I can become an uncle without undergoing any intrinsic change: I can do it unknowingly and in my sleep while my sister does all the work in a maternity ward across the country. Unlike uncle-hood, apparent-size may not seem changeable in this extrinsic fashion. But it is.

Q

66 *In upholding the concept of 'race', do we make racism possible?* **99**

A

Peter S. Fosl: Yes, I think we do – generally speaking.

For this reason, one of the purposes of philosophical interrogation of the concept of 'race' must be to undermine it. Aside from teaching about the genealogy of the concept of race and showing how it's more a social than a biological category, I have been experimenting with both minimising my use of racial terms and substituting 'lighter-skinned' and 'darker-skinned' when describing people. These terms, unlike 'black' or 'white' (which are binary and stark in their difference), are comparative and suggest both gradation and continuity (which I think are more accurate to the biological facts of the matter). Ethnic terms like 'African' are useful, too, but don't suggest inclusion and continuity quite as well. That said, I don't think the use of ethnic terms is terribly pernicious, except when their use is exceptional – that is, where ethnic terms are used to 'other', to single out in a demeaning way, to separate and subordinate. One has to be careful using them.

There are situations, however, where using racial concepts can serve morally desirable purposes. Cases where this is so typically involve using racial concepts to subvert themselves. Let me explain.

I've come to think that there's a certain kind of social reality to racial concepts. That is, I think that they exist in a deep way in our society, that they structure the way nearly all of us view the world, and that while they're ultimately not fixed or necessary, they're not going away anytime soon – and not without a lot of cultural and conceptual labour. Understanding this one might, for example, use the concept of 'race' as it exists in some contexts to advance affirmative action and diversity policies, to teach 'black' literature courses, to run anti-racism workshops, to analyse judicial decisions, to criticise housing and banking practices, to prosecute hate crimes etc. School population policies that use race as a factor may be used to undermine the concept and practices of race. So-called 'black' literature (as opposed to African literature) courses, too, may be enlisted to make themselves obsolete (or anyway meaningful in a different way). Again, rather than (simply) upholding 'race', these ways of using the concept can actually help to diminish or even eliminate it.

Of course, the blade does cut both ways. So even in these salutary roles, racial concepts can simultaneously uphold 'race' on one level while they undermine it on another. Taking steps to point out the problems with racial concepts and to undermine them whenever possible is, therefore, something that's very tricky, but it's also something, morally speaking, we really ought to try to do.

Q

66 *Is it morally wrong to want to marry only someone from your own ethnic group?* **99**

A

Peter S. Fosl: Simply put, no – not in itself.

I've come to this conclusion, however, only after a few troubling encounters with people close to me. I remember, for example, a darker-skinned (black) friend of mine objecting to her son's dating a lighter-skinned (white) woman. On another occasion, while my own son was playing with the daughter of some Jewish friends, I joked that someday we might be in-laws. They replied casually that it was important to them for their daughter to marry another Jew (at which point my son offered to convert). I was at first shocked by my friends' positions, and I'm still not without my criticisms. But I've come to appreciate their reasons, reasons that are especially compelling for those in minority groups.

Let's start with the bad reasons. Reasons for marrying *only* someone from one's own ethnic group may, of course, be immoral. For example, it would be immoral only to want to marry someone from one's own ethnic group in order to produce children belonging to that group so that an unjust supremacy may be preserved, especially the supremacy of an invasive and newly dominant population.

It would also be wrong, I think, to want to marry someone *only* because he or she belonged to one's ethnic group. It's preferable to consider other factors in marriage as well – like affection and compatibility. Moreover, all things being equal, it's better under many current social conditions to consider partners from other groups, as intermarriage can help subvert social tensions.

Note, in addition, that there's a difference between 'wanting' or 'desiring' only members of one's own group and limiting oneself to that group by repressing one's desires for those outside the group. Other things being equal, this sort of repression is morally undesirable.

On the other hand, in many circumstances I think taking ethnic background into consideration, as one factor among many, is morally permissible and even advisable. One's desire might be limited to a particular ethnicity because of one's self-knowledge – that is from a sense of one's personal requirements for compatibility. Limited desire might also flow from an appreciation of the beauties and excellences of one's ethnic traditions, rituals, etc. I think it morally defensible for minority groups, groups that are threatened, or groups that have been historically oppressed (Jews and blacks, for example) to consider ethnic background as a way of preserving their ethnic cultures.

In all this, however, I wish to be clear that there's a significant difference between an individual's wants, taking ethnicity into consideration, and going so far as to prohibit the wanting or the marrying of people across ethnic lines. The requirements of individual liberty ultimately trump the desire and even the duty to preserve ethnic groups.

Q

" *If someone judges her own life to be very negative, isn't it her right to terminate what has become an unpleasant existence – even if others do not believe her life is all that bad or without the prospect of improvement?*

Also, is it really fair to point to the harm that would befall others from her suicide as a reason for her not to kill herself? After all, isn't your life your own? **"**

A

Thomas Pogge: It *is* fair to point to the harms that would befall others from one's suicide, because such harms are surely not morally irrelevant. They are relevant, for example, when the potential suicide has caused others to be dependent on him or her. Consider, for example, a woman who has given birth to children whose lives are likely to be blighted by her suicide. To be sure, in many cases the fact that others would be harmed by a person's suicide is not this person's responsibility. It is not her responsibility, for instance, that she has parents or siblings who would be deeply upset by her suicide. But even in these cases, should she not at least do what she can to ease the pain of parents, siblings, friends, etc. left behind?

In these ways, perhaps suicide is not all that different from other actions people take. They may have a right to take these actions, in the sense that it would be wrong to prevent them from so acting; but this does not mean that such actions are beyond moral criticism. Their execution may be morally flawed in diverse ways, and sometimes these actions may be morally wrong altogether.

Thus, consider divorce. People have a moral right to walk out on a marriage in the sense that it would be wrong to prevent them from doing so. Nonetheless, people often walk out in ways that cause much avoidable pain and hardship to the spouse and children. And sometimes even the most considerate way of walking out would cause so much pain and hardship, for the sake of a relatively small gain, that the agent would do wrong to give precedence to his or her own happiness over that of his or her family. The important, general point here is this: even if one has a moral right to do X (i.e., it would be morally wrong for others to prevent one from doing X) one's doing X may still be morally wrong.

Q

Why don't people who say that when you die you go to a better place kill themselves? If death is a better place, why are they staying in this 'lesser' world?

A

Alexander George: Perhaps some people's confidence in an afterlife isn't strong enough to quell all their fears about death. Perhaps some don't wish to cause pain to their friends or loved ones, who will miss them terribly. And perhaps some believe that they don't have the right to quit their station in life (as John Locke put it): they are God's property and have no right to destroy themselves.

Q

66 *Why should we respect the dead?* **99**

A

Thomas Pogge: Here are three reasons to consider. First, we should respect the dead because they want to be respected. Sure, being dead, they do not want this now; but they did want it when they were alive. Imagine you have a certain deeply embarrassing secret that only your best friend knows. You very strongly want no one else to know. This fact gives your best friend a weighty reason not to tell others, even when she can do so in a way that you will never find out about. This reason may disappear if you no longer mind others knowing. But it persists when you die without having changed your mind – or so one could hold.

Second, we should respect the dead because doing so makes their lives better. The quality of our lives depends not merely on our mental states but also on our contributions to the world. These contributions can continue when we die: composers, artists and novelists enrich many lives even after they die, and this in turn makes their own lives more valuable. Not respecting the dead, e.g., by obliterating their work or memory, can cut off such posthumous contributions and thereby reduce the value of the dead person's life (relative to what it otherwise would have been).

Third, we should respect the dead because doing so is a practice from which the living benefit. Here I am not referring to the benefit of ourselves being respected after we die (else I would just be repeating the two earlier points). Rather, I am thinking of how we living would alter our conduct, in ways that are bad for all of us, if we believed that, once dead, we would no longer be respected. For example, would we expend much worry and effort on trying to ensure that our assets go where we want them to go? If a last will and testament cannot ensure this (because it would not be respected), then many will dispose of their assets before they die, often becoming very poor or dependent on support from friends, family or the state. So, you benefit now from the fact that you and others live in the secure knowledge that your/their last will is going to be respected. You benefit in that you need not worry about or implement the proper disposition of your assets now, and also in that you need not deal with the additional poverty and other problems that would result from others' early disposition of their assets.

One Last, But Not Final, Question

Q

“ *Why do philosophers make seemingly simple questions so complicated and confusing?* **”**

A

Alexander George: There is no reason to think that a simple question must have a simple answer. The question 'Why are there tides?' is very simple; a good answer to it is very complicated. (But maybe you think that typically the questions philosophers give complicated answers to *can* be answered simply!)

One might go on to wonder *why* simple questions often don't have simple answers. Well, that's a good simple question and I suspect it has no simple answer! Questions in philosophy often ask for an explanation, or rationalisation, of some belief of ours; for instance, a philosopher might want to know why we believe that other people are conscious (even though we can never experience, and so have direct evidence of, their consciousness). Now sometimes, a philosopher's notion of a good explanation is similar to that of a scientist's: an account that makes use of a few basic claims that eventually lead, through the process of inference, to many interesting and varied consequences. In other words, philosophers often look for *theories*, accounts that bring order to, or systematise, a range of previously unrelated phenomena by showing how they all follow from certain basic assumptions. And theories, because they seek to squeeze a lot of juice from just a few initial claims, can lead to complex chains of reasoning: the path from starting points to conclusions can be long and winding. This can seem – and indeed *be* – a complicated affair.

A

Nicholas D. Smith: There is an ancient saying (in Greek) – '*Chalepa ta kala*', meaning, 'Noble things are difficult'. Not all things that are valuable are difficult . . . but some are. And part of their value, I think, derives from the difficulty. In difficult endeavours, even the smallest successes are thrilling.

But here is another answer (also with ancient roots): Aristotle, in the beginning of his work, *Metaphysics*, says that 'philosophy begins in wonder'. I think that's right, and it is right about *any kind of inquiry at all*. But that means that producing results, in an inquiry, is going to be difficult – because in every serious inquiry, we begin in wonder. And we *wonder* because we are *ignorant*: if we already knew what we wondered about, we wouldn't wonder! Conquering ignorance is a tough business; as Socrates noted (in Plato's *Apology*), even *recognising* our own ignorance can be difficult . . . and is all too rare (then and now).

Contributors

Louise Antony teaches at the University of Massachusetts, Amherst.

Nalini Bhushan teaches at Smith College, Northampton, Massachusetts.

David Brink teaches at the University of California, San Diego.

Mark Crimmins teaches at Stanford University, Palo Alto, California.

Peter S. Fosl teaches at Transylvania University, Lexington, Kentucky.

Jyl Gentzler teaches at Amherst College, Amherst, Massachusetts.

Alexander George teaches at Amherst College, Amherst, Massachusetts.

Mitchell S. Green teaches at the University of Virginia, Charlottesville.

Sean Greenberg teaches at Johns Hopkins University, Baltimore, Maryland.

Richard Heck teaches at Brown University, Providence, Rhode Island.

Amy Kind teaches at Claremont McKenna College, Claremont, California.

Marc Lange teaches at the University of North Carolina, Chapel Hill.

Oliver Leaman teaches at the University of Kentucky, Lexington.

Peter Lipton teaches at the University of Cambridge.

Joseph G. Moore teaches at Amherst College, Amherst, Massachusetts.

Thomas Pogge teaches at Columbia University, New York City.

Gabriel Segal teaches at King's College London.

Matthew Silverstein teaches at the University of Michigan, Ann Arbor.

Nicholas D. Smith teaches at Lewis and Clark College, Portland, Oregon.

Mark Sprevak teaches at the University of Cambridge.

Sharon Street teaches at New York University, New York City.

Daniel J. Velleman teaches at Amherst College, Amherst, Massachusetts.

Acknowledgments

I extend my sincerest thanks to colleagues, near and far, without whose unstinting help this project would have remained in the realm of non-being, and to Amherst College for all its very generous support. Finally, as ever, my gratitude to friends and family, for whom I had many more questions than appear in this book.

A.G.